Leon Haller is a small-business consultant who teaches business finance at the University of Massachusetts in Boston. He conducts seminars on the subject of planning and financial management at the Cambridge Center for Adult Education and other organizations in the Boston area. He is Technical Assistance Coordinator of the Massachusetts Accountants in the Public Interest, Inc.

FINANCIAL RESOURCE MANAGEMENT FOR NONPROFIT ORGANIZATIONS

LEON HALLER

A SPECTRUM BOOK

PRENTICE-HALL, INC., Englewood Cliffs, New Jersey 07632

658.15

H 185

Library of Congress Cataloging in Publication Data

Haller, Leon.
    Financial resource management for nonprofit
    organizations.

    "A Spectrum Book."
    Bibliography: p.
    Includes index.
    1. Corporations, Nonprofit—Finance.
I. Title.
HG4027.65.H34 1982   658.1'5   82-10174
ISBN 0-13-316307-5
ISBN 0-13-316299-0 (pbk.)

This book is available
at a special discount when ordered in large quantities.
Contact Prentice-Hall, Inc., General Publishing
Division, Special Sales, Englewood Cliffs, N.J. 07632.

10 9 8 7 6 5 4 3 2 1

ISBN 0-13-316307-5

ISBN 0-13-316299-0 {PBK.}

Prentice-Hall International, Inc., *London*
Prentice-Hall of Australia Pty. Limited, *Sydney*
Prentice-Hall Canada Inc., *Toronto*
Prentice-Hall of India Private Limited, *New Delhi*
Prentice-Hall of Japan, Inc., *Tokyo*
Prentice-Hall of Southeast Asia Pte. Ltd., *Singapore*
Whitehall Books Limited, *Wellington, New Zealand*

*To Uncle Sig
and all my family*

Contents

vii

Preface

This book presents a comprehensive yet practical understanding of the role of financial management in small nonprofit organizations. Its most important feature is that it uses nontechnical, everyday language to explain financial problems and organizing tasks common to a wide variety of nonprofit organizations, including cooperative enterprises.

The book provides the reader with a clear guide for planning activities before seeking funds and for understanding how to handle money after it has been obtained. It illustrates how to think about resource needs, how to translate them into useful budgets, and how to organize the management tasks necessary to provide simple controls over expenditures. It also shows how an uncomplicated financial operating report done on a timely basis can help prevent the many financial crises that are common experiences in small nonprofit organizations. In general, it demystifies and simplifies what seem to be complex concepts and activities.

Solid guidelines for the tasks of board members, managers, staff, bookkeepers, and accountants are presented, as is an explanation of the interdependence of their financial management functions and responsibilities. This helps people better understand their jobs and those of others in the organization, thus making possible a considerable reduction of wasteful efforts and confusion about who makes financial decisions. The book provides board members of small organizations with an understanding of what the role of the treasurer is, and tells them how they can help prevent important financial problems for which they are ultimately accountable.

A picture of the manager's or executive director's financial administration responsibilities is presented in a way that will allow that person to recognize and to arrange administrative tasks in the organization and to deal with the financial concerns of outside agencies and funding sources. The book helps board members and administrators understand that the priorities of financial management are inseparable from and of equal importance to those of program management.

Important new themes about small, private nonprofit organizations underlie this book. They are of significant value because they look at such organizations in a nontraditional, more up-to-date way. This book points out that the nonprofit organization is

1. *An innovative force in the economy.* To a great extent, small nonprofit organizations are innovators of services, management structure, and new products that are valuable to the needs of our society. Consequently, the promotion and understanding of their financial administration requirements among people who work in them and of funding sources that support them is critical to the vital role that they play.

2. *Managers of resources, not charity distributors.* It is time to rethink and redefine the economic role of private nonprofit organizations in our society. Billions of dollars pass through them for the purpose of meeting diverse needs of the population. To see them as business operations that produce services and products to meet unfilled needs is to focus on the management and productive use of resources. Thus the question of "profitability" is not particularly relevant. The labels of "profit" and "charity" both obscure the issues of the management translating ideas into effective results or our attempts to translate our ideas into meaningful results.

3. *Organization functions, not form, comprise effective financial management.* It is not how the organization's efforts are organized—on a traditional basis with a board of directors "on top" and workers "on the bottom" of the decision-making ladder, or a collective of owner/consumers who make all decisions together—but what financial management jobs need to be done and how the different functions of planning, purchasing, recording, and reporting information are interrelated, that determines effective management. Regardless of the type of organization, managerial tasks are assignable, if

they are known and understood, and individuals can be held accountable to the organization for doing or not doing their part to advance its purposes.

The unique approach of this book is that financial management problems within nonprofit organizations are explained in a way that can be easily understood by the manager or anyone else in the organization. For example, though the chapter on financial reporting is presented with a view that integrates the needs of project managers, board members, and funding source administrators, no special or professional training is required to produce this information. There is no "mystique" to using financial tools, since they represent measures of how we plan and use resources.

The topics discussed throughout the book are treated as managerial rather than concerns of the finance and accounting "professional." The most important feature of this book is that familiar topics and problems are combined in a unifying perspective that can be understood by everyone. The subjects are sequentially presented to follow a natural flow of the jobs and responsibilities of different people working together in an organization.

Because of the rapid growth of cooperative enterprises in recent years, and the formation of the National Consumers Cooperative Bank, the book also focuses on basic concepts of small-business finance, including the nature of commercial risk, subsidized financing, and breakeven analysis. These are explored within the context of special financial and managerial conditions of cooperative organization. This book translates and applies commercial and financial concepts to the activities of cooperatives.

The objectives of this book are (1) to provide an operating framework for managers and board members so they can better understand the financial administration of the organization, as well as their individual roles and responsibilities for its programs and activities; (2) to fill a serious gap in the educational and training needs of people who are involved in the management of small nonprofit organization; and (3) to emphasize that understanding the financial management component of a small organization is critical to its well-being because this supports and strengthens the morale of those struggling to implement its purposes.

The scope of the material is broad but unifying. It shows financial planning as a derivative of careful activities planning, financial controls in terms of functions rather than authority, and financial integrity as a result of people doing different jobs in an organized and understandable way. Much of the confusion about this subject is dispelled in the book. As a result, readers will be prepared to deal with the financial management dimension of their jobs and thereby find their vital work more productive and challenging.

ACKNOWLEDGMENTS

It is my pleasure to express my thanks to the many people who have helped me with this book in the past two and a half years. All my family and friends, and many of my associates and students have had a hand in helping me prepare these pages. In particular, four people offered thoughtful and valuable criticism. Steve Herman, fellow co-op member and CPA with Arthur Andersen & Co. in Boston, and Molly Lovelock, teacher and consultant to small organizations on bookkeeping systems, were most instrumental in helping me produce a useful book. Didi Stevens not only taught me much about the English language, but helped me in the general task of writing this book. Later on, Paul Hessel introduced me to the legal intricacies of publishing contracts.

Very important to the expression of the ideas in the following pages have been the opportunities to share and understand the dimensions of this material by teaching at the Cambridge Adult Education Center, the Policy Training Center, and Lesley College Graduate School, all in Cambridge, Massachusetts. Many thoughtful and exciting people involved in a diversity of nonprofit organizations participated in my seminars and courses and provided valuable input. Teaching finance and business analysis at University of Massachusetts, College of Management and Professional Sciences, gave me an opportunity to think more carefully about the nature and meaning of the terms "financial management" and "organization." I also owe many thanks to co-workers at the MASS Accountants for the Public Interest, Inc., who provide technical assistance to small nonprofit organizations, as well as to friends and co-workers involved in the Cambridge Food Cooperative and the co-op movement in New England.

Della Hardy provided exceptionally valuable editorial work, as did Susan Himmelfarb, while Fred Cowan, Director of Finance for the Boston Children's Service Association, and Debra Knox, career consultant, helped review the final version. John Hooven, good friend and management consultant, deserves much credit for assisting me in translating my experiences with "boards" and "planning." A special thank you for encouragement during difficult times goes to my brother Jerry, Penny Axelrod, Sandra Carnesale, and Erica Harth, June Namias, and Lindy Sutton.

Above all is my endless appreciation to Jeanne Saint-Gelais for the hard work of typing and the real enjoyment of working together.

FINANCIAL RESOURCE MANAGEMENT FOR NONPROFIT ORGANIZATIONS

I

SIGNIFICANCE AND POTENTIAL OF SMALL NONPROFIT ORGANIZATIONS

1

The Private
Nonprofit Organization

IMPORTANCE AND DEFINITION

There are more than 500,000 private nonprofit organizations regis-
tered with the Internal Revenue Service as tax exempt, but there
are probably another 250,000 to 300,000 that are probably eligi-
ble. This total number includes a relatively small group of large
organizations with which this book is not concerned. For most of
them, the scope and impact of their activities is usually local.
These organized efforts are the primary focus of this book.

Small, private nonprofit (public service) organizations, with
roughly up to $1 million of revenues, are generally created and
managed by people with considerable enthusiasm and belief for
"what needs to be done" but little business background and interests. They are the channels through which innumerable local services and public action movements are produced. If we shed the
burden of labels such as "charity," "good works," "welfare,"
"helping," "stewardship," "grantsmanship," and "volunteerism"
and look closely at small, private nonprofit organizations, their
activity is quite familiar. These groups and the individuals who
promote them have a significant "entrepreneurial" role in our

society. They try to mobilize resources to effect change by organizing new services to meet unmet needs, locally and sometimes nationally. They often fill an important gap between the private profit-making sector and the government sector at all levels. The entrepreneurial spirit manifest in the initiatives and the creativity of their actions and accomplishments is very much a part of a traditional energy and leadership of change in America.

STRENGTH AND STRUGGLE OF INNOVATING ORGANIZATIONS

By looking at the diverse productivity of the private nonprofit sector, you can see that the "business" of these private organizations is to a great extent developing innovative services and products (including information dissemination and organizational structures)—new ways to explore and resolve problems of education, human services, cultural expression, the organization of production, and the marketing of consumer goods and services.

What are the characteristics of small nonprofit organizations? Like all entrepreneurial endeavors, profit or nonprofit, considerable amounts of *voluntarily provided resources* are rechanneled into potentially productive use. Those resources are from the pockets and hard work of families, friends, many communities, and interest groups. The resources are mobilized by a relatively limited paid staff. Furthermore, the *environment is highly competitive*, with many groups or promoters often vying for the same sources of funding. Some funding sources have established priorities among the types of projects they will support. But even when the seeker of funds is matched with the funding sources in terms of mutual interest, there is still competition, plenty of it.

The term *shoestring financing* usually is applied to new profit-making organizations, but it is the same for all start-ups. They are "underfinanced," but many survive and grow in spite of lack of funds. And as they grow, their financial problems shift to planning and control over the funds and resources that they have. Another typical characteristic of entrepreneurial efforts is that *skills are learned "on the job."* Most people who are initially involved in promoting and developing an organization are doing it because of personal and professional motivation or beliefs. They are generally not selling management skills; there is little to pay for already acquired skills. They are rarely managers with organizational skills and functions. Their skills consist of the ability to launch ideas and convince others to support them. Finally, formal structures, such as boards of directors and corporate officers, are *organized as legal formalities*, rather than perceived in terms of organizational needs or functional roles, when people are getting activities started and developed. Persons who are typically involved in these roles often don't know what they should be doing or what is expected other than supporting a leader who is promoting the initial ideas and efforts.

NONPROFIT: CHARITY OR MAINSTREAM?

Historically, the private nonprofit sector appears to have been looked upon as a depository for the support of good causes and Christian action. The focus was more on the donor–donee relationship. In the last two decades, however, a greater emphasis of mutuality has developed. Federal and state government agencies have expanded their utilization of the private nonprofit organization through contractual relationships. They have facilitated efforts of the poor and of minority groups to become represented in local services. These agencies have financed a considerable number of locally sponsored programs that have proven their social and economic worth in solving some problems that neither the traditional government activities nor the private profit-making sectors have been able to do. Whereas in the past most nonprofit organizations were voluntary, primarily attracting only those upper-middle-class women who had an interest in "charitable" activities, there are now many paying jobs of professional status. The relationship has shifted considerably between the paid staff and the unpaid volunteers, female and male, who are now from all age groups and economic classes.

Because the relationship between funding sources and organizations has gradually shifted, concerns about management have been surfacing in the sector. How has this come about?

Measurement of Productivity and Managerial Competence

First, for a long time, no one had expected or tried to measure *productivity* or *managerial competency*. However, in the past decade with increased emphasis of public sector and local government agencies on using the private sector, particularly the small local service agency, expectations have begun to change. As the flow of government funds increased into the private, traditionally charity-oriented environment, both the questions about and the functions of management of resources have become manifest. Instead of donations to good causes and charity toward the poor, the greatest funding influence is now found in the "purchase of services" contracts, integrated services planning, development and matching grants, and an increasing changeover from direct federal administration to state and local control. With these changes has also come a greater emphasis on "accountability," more reliable and useful financial reporting systems, and reimbursement contracting procedures. Many states have been considering more stringent liability conditions for officers and board members of private nonprofit organizations in an attempt to emphasize the seriousness of their financial responsibilities. Greater managerial sophistication about such matters as rate setting, delivery systems models, information systems, cost controls, and so forth is required of managers today.

There are now many courses and books on "grantsmanship," the how-to of getting private and public funds for nonprofit activities and programs. This training deals with the shaping of proposals and their marketing to government agencies, private corporations, foundations, and the general public. Large numbers of grants seekers and staff of various new and old human service programs, community activities, and research and education organizations in all areas of the social, economic, political, and cultural life of the nation have been the audiences of this new learning. Indeed, conveying ideas about how to obtain money is a big and profitable business.

Need for Management Training and Technical Assistance

Unfortunately, newer financial and managerial expectations of small nonprofit organizations by state and local funding sources have not been matched by *management training and technical assistance* from any source. Regional and state cultural funding organizations wonder why there is such a high rate of collapse among the organizations they support, even though they put considerable effort into sponsoring training programs for developing fund-raising techniques. Only in recent times is there a growing idea that getting money and managing its use might be perceived more accurately as separate issues. Furthermore, though nongovernment sources have been increasingly expected or assumed to be ready to provide matching funds and other contributions, it is only on rare occasions, if at all, that the diverse funding sources of corporate, foundation, and government entities ever meet to have a general discussion about management issues and training needs of the organizations they support. The overall funding mentality is still focused on getting and giving money.

Attention to the
Role of Governance

Another and more subtle issue of management is the role of *governance* of small organizations. There is more often than not an assumption among established funding sources that because a small service or cultural organization has a board of directors, especially with a well-known name on it, "management" exists. So, the funding sources view the "real" issues of ability of the recipient organizations to provide services as problems outside the social and economic order of the day, not possibly in the microcosm of the organizational guidance itself. Board members and advisory groups, rather than taking on the responsibility of assuring themselves of objective information, financial planning and review, policy development, and overall supervision, usually involve themselves in a passive and often image-loaded experience. Most of them are unprepared to ask:

1. How is money being spent?
2. What are the financial and planning needs that will allow us to achieve the goals that our organization pursues?

Misplaced Ideological Attitude

Equally serious is the problem of what seems to be a cultural influence of the "halo effect." This is an *ideological attitude* that often permeates the minds of staff, advisors, and financial supporters of private nonprofit organizations and many cooperative business enterprises. One of its most obvious manifestations is the tendency to associate the concepts of managerial tools and simple levels of accountability with crude, negative stereotypes of "business" and "profits." Too often, visions of unwholesomeness are somehow evoked by the idea that a small, private nonprofit organization is a type of (service) business whose management requirements are not very different from any other type of activity involving people and money. Thus for many participants in the sector, "higher values" than monetary assignments are or have to be used to measure outcome or make organizational policy. Plans and planning, costs of resources, "job responsibility," and so on often become subjects of a morality play. The business of management of an organization's activities and the management of the finances takes a second place (if it takes *any* place) to "moral issues" of purpose and procedure until a serious financial crisis occurs. And it invariably does. This attitude ultimately undermines attempts to make a serious, long-term impact on meeting a need in a community; moreover, it significantly reduces the potential effective use of available resources. It often contributes to exploitive wage and salary practices, as well as a failure to recognize the need to pay for developed and specialized managerial skills, particularly financial ones.

INNOVATORS, MANAGERS, AND INVESTORS

In private profit-making organizations, profits are generally but not completely a barometer of good management practices. If management is inadequate or incompetent, losses usually result and investors step in to make changes. Losses are a direct concern and provocation to investors. Sales (market acceptance) to consumers, either public or industry, constitute a measure of the validity of the product idea or service. If market acceptance is unresponsive, the idea as it was developed is not validated in the marketplace. This applies to the local store as well as the products of multimillion-dollar corporations. Investors, managers, and consumers are linked. In the situation in which the manager is also a prime investor, as in many small businesses and new enterprises, successful idea development and investor decision making are intertwined. When the developers of new ventures seek private-sector investors, the latter usually require that the developers put their own money into their projects as both an incentive and protection through sharing risk of their management decisions. The same is true of borrowing from commercial banks.

Grants seekers and their funding sources, both private and public, seem more like unequal partners. They have a rich man-beggar relationship, somehow promoted in the name of the public interest. While both may be motivated by the potential of producing some benefit for society through the promotion of a new program or even the support of traditional charitable cause, this uneasy relationship and its mentality pervade much of the atmosphere of the private nonprofit sector. The fact is that organizing and management efforts are not different in the private nonprofit realm from those in the profit-making sector, though the words and labels to describe them might be. Operational and financial plans have to be developed, and financing arranged. Resources are acquired and converted into services and products for "clients" or consumers. The fact that profits are made or not is incidental when one compares the development of workable ideas, management functions, and financial organization tasks. The risks that idea developers and implementers present to funding sources—unworkable projects, and poor managerial ability to utilize resources effectively—are common among all small organizations and business enterprises.

Thus, to support improvements in management of the resources used by organizations in the nonprofit sector is to enrich society. The development of capable management and productive organization is a critical focus for all who are involved with small nonprofit organizations. These organizations comprise the medium for lasting change and community benefits to the society. Such benefits are the societal "profits" generated by investment in the private nonprofit sector. Thus, to see that human and financial resources are not misdirected in organizing and implementing new concepts is as necessary as an "investment" focus as is supporting the ideas themselves.

In this context it is not surprising to find that the same problems and conditions which characterize small, private nonprofit organizations also describe their counterpart of the private profit-making endeavors. The chief cause of their demise is poor business and financial planning and lack of understanding of the managerial needs and functions. Because the *entrepreneurial orientation* is usually one of promoting new ideas and organizing new efforts, the core of the entrepreneurial effort and spirit is "getting started." The less dramatic area of careful evaluation of plans, estimation of costs, use of financial controls, and organization of tasks of continued operations still must be dealt with. This is the managing perspective, a matter of getting the most productive use out of actual and potentially available resources. Consciousness about managing resources is what creates a longer-term impact on society's needs, both large and small. Both "getting started" and "managing" activities are of equal "worth" and inseparable consideration, though skills requirements are quite different. The relationship between getting started and management in terms of financial planning and controls is the underlying orientation of this book.

The next three chapters explore the meaning of PLANNING in the context of organizing people's efforts, formulating programs, and translating both into dollars and sense. They describe functions that are essential to the financial management component of implementation of any organization's concerns and character.

PLANNING
AND BUDGET
FORMULATION

2

The Business of
Financial Organization

Many projects and organizations start with very little public support in terms of money and direction. Their beginnings are characterized by the intense personal efforts of a few people trying to get a few dollars here and there for their particular issue or service. The ideas of "management" and "organization" come about much later or are forced upon them as more people get involved, and often when the potential for using more resources is perceived and pursued. There is no particular connection or indicator for when one level of promotional effort is transformed into another. Increased funding does not necessarily spark the sense of "getting organized." However, as more and more resources are used to implant a response to an unmet need, someone inevitably asks, "What is the best way to make an impact, and how can we get more money (to acquire the resources) to do it?" These basic questions are what "planning" is all about. They are applicable regardless of whether activities are profit making or nonprofit, incorporated or not, "radical" or "traditional," communal or national.

13

Most people who start activities eventually have to reach out beyond their own resource capabilities of time and money. In so doing, they request others—their friends, supporters, and associates—to believe in their projects and goals. Such requests, either verbal or written, often imply or actually state a rationale for the value of what they are trying to do, and might indicate some vague "plan" for using funds. "We believe in. . . . Please assist our efforts with your money to organize research, treat, advocate, teach, publicize, etc." What usually is experienced in going beyond an immediate audience and source of funds is an increased requirement to develop some type of defined picture of what the activity is now, and what it will accomplish or produce in the future if additional funding provides added resources. The more institutional the funding sources are, the more they require a minimal proof of the applicant being a public entity or organized effort such as a legally chartered corporation with a board of directors or trustees. Actual or potential tax exemption status is also important, because of the tax consequences on the donor's or grantor's participation. Validation of activities by independent groups or individuals may also be required. Professional groups, users, sponsors often attest to the need for your activities. Sometimes included in this condition is financial verification of past expenditures in the form of annual financial reports prepared by an accountant. These are often the stipulations to obtaining a review of a funding request or proposal submittal. But provisions vary considerably with the many different sources. In the commercial world, suppliers of trade credits, commercial bank loans, and investors have their diverse conditions too, all related to their purposes, operating procedures, and the levels of risk they will undertake in permitting you to use their resources.

PLANNING AND "ORGANIZATION"

As a day-to-day reality, as activities expand, the need for some type of order for making decisions and using resources often becomes evident and desirable. More and more people are involved in carrying out the functions and tasks that comprise the activities. Without coordination of individual efforts, people who work toward the same goals do not know what others are doing. They often become confused about their own roles and contributions, as well as have conflicts with others. Thus "organization" refers to the interrelationships which make diverse jobs more effective through conscious design, or planning.

Planning is a dynamic and constant function of organized effort. It necessarily involves continuous review of past conditions and actions so that new decisions can be made that are relevant to current knowledge or perceptions about what is being done or should be done. It is a matter of creating a framework to take action in the future in some coordinated way. Often, planning includes making explicit many of the procedures that we might perform informally. Through delegation or assignment, responsibilities for implementing individual tasks are made known, agreed upon, and are capable of being shared. Organizational functions and relationships with others can be expressly established, independent of personal relationships.

So when someone asks, "What is the best way to make an impact?" you ultimately answer with a list of practical steps that are essential to implementing an activity or groups of activities. The coordination of those functions, both administrative and programmatic, according to a mutually agreed set of priorities, produces organizational design, a picture of (hoped-for) integrated efforts. The design is tested and modifiable through implementation and review. As long as planning is an ongoing activity, results of past action are reintegrated into operations. Consequently, organizational form is derived from actual tasks and functions being carried out or that should be undertaken.

All this is to say that "organization" is not a fixed concept. It grows and changes as activities grow and change. Its design at any given time also reflects both legal and operational influences of ownership and trusteeship, managerial and technical resource requirements, financial controls, and funding conditions. The substance of an organizational design or "structure" is fluid and functional rather than predetermined and academic. Most of all, this view is a reminder to all of us that we work together to actualize shared goals in a constantly changing setting, among varying and often unknown conditions.

OVERVIEW OF SKILLS REQUIREMENTS

In going from a small activity that uses a few thousand dollars a year to an organized effort that will involve many thousands or hundreds of thousands of dollars, the acquisition and development of different managerial and technical skills is required to effectively plan and implement programs.

Common to all organizations, profit or nonprofit, public or private, are these basic categories of management activities:

Financing.	Obtaining, controlling, and "accounting for" money that passes through the organization.
Production.	Acquiring, coordinating, supervising the conversion of human and material resources into goods and services.
Marketing.	Selling and delivering goods and services to current and potential users, and assessing the effect of the availability and use of your output on the consuming public.

Each one of these categories can be further subdivided and detailed into component tasks. Planning, deciding what courses of action to take, and review—assessing what has happened—are functions that occur in each and at all organizational levels. As a united action, planning is the organizational mainspring that links the present and the future, and daily decisions to the reason for the organization and particular use of resources.

FINANCIAL MANAGEMENT ELEMENTS

The financial management activities in nonprofit organizations, exclusive of fund raising, are commonly referred to as treasury functions. In a corporate structure, the treasurer is specifically and ultimately responsible for the financial health of an organization. Whether or not there is a legally designated person with that title is not important. The governance committees, officers, and most managers appreciate that carrying out and supervising financial administration tasks is critical to the continuation of the life of an organization, regardless of its form or purpose. Figure 1 illustrates the basic components of the treasurer's role.

The essential functions of developing and maintaining financial integrity for whatever an organization does are:

- Seeing that all financial transactions are recorded
- Controlling the use of the assets of the organization
- Assuring that accurate financial reports are prepared
- Anticipating financial problems
- Complying with state and federal reporting requirements

While the ultimate financial management responsibility may rest with the person or role of the "treasurer," as a matter of fact,

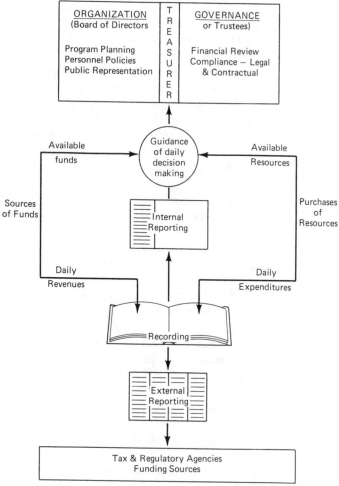

FIGURE 1. The treasurer's role.

these functions and the many specific tasks that compose them are delegated to the executive director, manager, or coordinator—whoever is in charge of activities on a daily basis. They in turn may be delegated to others involved in financial controls and information management—the business manager or bookkeeper—and those who may have authority to make spending decisions such as project coordinators and their assistants. Because some tasks are delegated does not mean that they are out of sight and out of mind. What it does mean is establishing specific links between tasks and people, having controls over the implementation of activity plans and their corresponding budgets.

Underlying these functions is the need to carry them out

17

simply and accurately in a reasonably orderly way. Financial planning in and of itself is an essential element of organizational and project control; it helps anticipate financial problems. Spending controls over most purchases are a matter of simple and functional checks and balances between budgeted amounts and decisions to spend, rather than wasted time and paper in seeking "authorizations" (financial plans). Reporting tells what has happened, so it has to provide a financial story about income and expenditures in such a way as to be understandable and useable for everyone involved. Thus all financial transactions should be recorded on a regular basis, and in consistent language. In certain instances, reporting is also a matter of "regulation" and contractual obligation. So the same information may have to be translatable into someone else's terms and format. Translations are not always easy. They sometimes require the expertise of an accountant, particularly when tax information is necessary and when formal accounting reports are required. Accountants can provide the independent assessment of financial records for all parties.

The basic financial management requirement is to have the financial data in a useable form. As such, it is the measure of the flow of resources into and out of the organization. The jobs of the bookkeeper and the accountant are to gather and organize, respectively, the data of all transactions of the organization so that information can be effectively utilized in the decisions of the managers and governance committees. Insofar as an organization uses funds that belong to others or have a public nature, then officers and governance members are also responsible for providing information to these funding sources (grantors, contractors, and investors), government regulatory agencies, and often, users/clients and community representatives.

3

Project Formulation

TURNING IDEAS INTO
AN ACTION FRAMEWORK

The innovative spirit usually associated with small companies in the for-profit sector, entrepreneurship, is manifest throughout the private sector in different organizational and economic forms. People who act to make their ideas and concerns public, and who try to effect an impact on the thoughts and lives of others, are entrepreneurs in the private nonprofit as well as the profit-making sector. This spirit is a creative, dynamic response to a situation in our economy, society, or a condition of our lives. We see all kinds of new activities that incorporate this spirit in the nonprofit sector. The new and organized efforts to educate the public about nuclear power or the disappearance of whales and other endangered wildlife; specialized services for the handicapped; economic development through local development corporations; "alternative" education; small publications in the arts; community cultural organizations such as musical groups and local theater; consumer and producer cooperatives of all types. The list is endless.

19

Both private and public sectors are sources for financing ideas. Through personal and corporate tax exemption, government contracting preferences, and separate legal recognition of nonprofit organizations, considerable financial support for ideas and services that will benefit the public is available. The task of the idea developers is to find individuals and organizational funding sources that will believe that the organization's goal or program concept is a worthwhile attempt to make an impact on the local community or the larger society in which we live. Thus, initial financing basically involves "selling" a concept about services, products, and organizations to potential "investors" in or buyers of nonprofit activities.

Many government agencies, under legislative direction, must carry out their activities through grants and purchase of services from private nonprofit organizations, rather than expand their own operations and payroll. As new public needs are revealed or crises take shape, the types of services change or have a different emphasis. For example, in the field of alcohol abuse much more attention is being focused on female drinkers than in the past because of the sharp rise in the incidence of alcohol abuse among this population during the past ten years.

Public support shifts with new ways of understanding and responding to social and economic conditions. The U.S. Congress expresses changes and emphasis in national priorities in new legislation. An example of a significant federal government direction in supporting the private nonprofit sector is the formation of the National Consumers' Cooperative Bank. Its purpose is to provide specialized credit and technical assistance to the rapidly growing activities of cooperatively owned business enterprises and housing throughout the country. The legislation passed by Congress in 1979 said that "the National Consumer Cooperative Bank will promote comparable growth of consumer cooperatives throughout the American economy, resulting in reduced inflation and people-oriented economic development. To accomplish this, the legislation: establishes a bank to make loans at market interest rates to cooperatives in a variety of fields; creates a Self-Help Development Fund and Technical Assistance capability to assist low-income cooperatives or cooperatives with special needs" (summary from the statement of "Proposed Policy" NCCB—January 1980). One of the general objectives is that the bank be "sensitive and responsive to the needs of cooperatives that are new, that service low-income persons, that utilize nontraditional management techniques, or that have been deprived of credit in the past."

The principles and concepts about the design and operation of the specific service project presented here apply to most situations that involve developing new activities in large organizations or promoting small ones in whatever field of services, cultural activities, or public advocacy. Any idea that responds to a specific social or economic condition is directly translatable into a plan of action. A financial plan and funding proposals are a further outcome of clarifying what you want to do and what you need from investors or purchasers of your services or products.

Let's say that you are employed in a family counseling center, partly funded by the Department of Mental Health in your state. The facilities serve a town of 45,000 residents. You know through your work as a counselor that child abuse problems exist, but in your agency and other organizations, there is no specific focus on services to this population. From conversations with medical professionals and some police contacts, you have determined that there seems to be a much greater incidence of child abuse than the public and city officials realize. There would be no problem collecting information on cases and making a professional assessment of the situation. Recently, a headline in the local newspaper was about the death of a three-year-old child who "unmistakably" died from physical violence. The city council, urged and supported by your state's Department of Mental Health, is suddenly ready to provide funding for some type of child abuse services. The president of the largest local manufacturing company expresses enlightened community interest with an offer of funds and other assistance to help in doing something in his town. You realize that here is an opportunity to do something about an "unmet need" in the community. You have your own professional motivation to get a clearer picture of the causes as well as help reduce the incidence of child abuse. There are others who are concerned with the problem.

Project "Justification"

When you start to take your ideas to others to create support, you offer arguments or justifications for what you want to do and what you think needs to be done. Essentially, you are defining a "market" for the services or products you intend to establish or

21

produce. Sometimes elaborate investigations are required in the form of research or "needs assessments" in order to attract interest and create an elementary reception from a potential funding source. In other instances, preparation of simple statistics or a carefully stated view of why the world is not flat as conventional wisdom presumes is all that appears necessary to win others over to your views and plans of action.

While governmental and other institutional sources often require fairly detailed justifications and plans for actions, especially for large projects, there are many other sources that do not. The ways to convince sources to believe in your organization's goals or approach to an unmet need and that it deserves funding, are quite diverse. In the example just given there is a distinct interest (priority) on the part of the Department of Mental Health to fund a project. There is also a documentable unmet need, the magnitude of which could be defined, that initially may justify the action and particular level of funding by the department.

There are other situations that are not nor initially need to be so clearly definable, such as many of the public advocacy programs. However, what is most important is that the purpose(s) of an organization or organized efforts be translatable to the "outside world" and information about the "unmet need" it serves be continuously sifted and measured whenever possible. Regardless of the form of presentations to funding sources, an organization's plans for action depend upon what its leaders see is the problem and what they determine should be done. Impetus of an organized effort is defined from within an organization. Funding sources require justifications or rationales for why they should allocate funds according to their needs, requirements, and politics.

Often funding sources themselves solicit ideas about how to solve a problem which they have outlined, or how to achieve specific results that they want to see. A regional office of the Law Enforcement Assistance Agency (LEAA), part of the Justice Department, requested proposals for training of the staff of youth services agencies in Massachusetts. The specific training was for improving the management skills of small, local organizations so that they could be more efficient and longer-lasting conduits of federal and state programs aimed at youth with problems. Part of LEAA funds were available for programs to youth who were or would probably be in trouble with law enforcement agencies in the state. This particular project asked for specific educational programs for what the agency had already determined was a management training need of its current and potential contractors carrying out its own goals.

How you present the verification of the unmet need in your proposals for funding varies with the interest and requirements of diverse funding sources, both individual and institutional. Of course your own talents for packaging and persuasion may sometimes be important ingredients for convincing some potential supporters, but much more substance is usually needed. As challenging as the art and technique ("grantsmanship") of seeking and obtaining financial support may be, the subject of the following pages is not how to justify your proposal or to raise money. However, since that activity may be an integral part of your efforts to plan and start a project, much of the following material, in fact, shows the connection between proposal development, financial planning, and relationships with funding sources. More important than grantsmanship skills (which are part of the organizational marketing functions), having good ideas, sound action plans, management capabilities, and related experience are usually the critical components of attracting funding sources.

Determine Goals/Define Strategy

A goal is a general statement of purpose of your project or organization. It answers the question of what you expect to accomplish by your efforts. In this case, your goals may be to provide a program of prevention and intervention services. Other goals for a child abuse project could be to research the dimension and causes of the problem; to train professionals, such as doctors, teachers, nurses, police, and family counselors; to coordinate all local human services providers; to act as an advocate for changing laws. A document of incorporation requires a statement of purpose, the legal equivalent of an organization's goal. That statement may be very general or specific about the purpose of the organization's activities.

An elaboration of how to best achieve the purpose(s) is a rationale or strategy which links all your activities. You carefully consider why your mousetrap will work differently and better than others in the market. Consequently, your strategy may be defined in context of existing or even planned activities of other organizations. You cannot focus on establishing criteria for selecting activities and making a priority for their implementation until you have defined a strategy for how you and others will go about effecting change. Suppose you determine that in this community there is neither broad knowledge of the problem of child abuse nor a place that people would contact for help if they thought they needed it. A publicity campaign and a hotline might therefore rank high on your list of possible activities if your strategy is based on public education. If a town hotline already exists, then you might design a publicity program to use this existing facility. There may be valid reasons for a separate hotline, but you must substantiate them. To clarify strategy design, differences in activities, and ultimately the resource requirements, you must carefully ask yourself, Is what I want to do a possible duplication of other activities or services? The answers are in terms of these dimensions:

- Who is your "market"? (Unmet needs)
- How do you reach it? (Strategy)
- What are you going to do that someone else does not do? (Uniqueness)

Select Activities Options

What are the possible activities for a new program of child abuse prevention and intervention? A hotline and referral office; a program to coordinate community mental health efforts with police, hospital and schools; a public awareness program; a grandmothers' helper club; a child rights and advocacy program; temporary foster-home care, a parents' COPE program and support group? The possibilities are endless. Each could have a different effect on the community and a different impact on the problem. Without a general statement of goals and a strategy for reaching them, this question of "Which activities should be considered?" has little meaning. Furthermore, without a guiding strategy for your program operations, a sense of priority cannot be incorporated into decisions about and commitment to the choice of activities.

Many activities are interrelated and support one another because of a particular organization strategy. A mental health hotline connected with emergency counseling facilities is very different from a hotline that only provides outside, professional referrals. If project activities are primarily for screening and reference, is there enough attention given to coordination with existing outside services? Can those services respond to the changes in client population that your activities may induce? If not, what activities should you plan to include in your program, and at what level of priority of both time and money?

Planning: A Functional Approach

The important work is to identify the functions that compose each activity, and to determine the resources necessary to carry them out. In the case of the hotline, telephones are required, along with office space, chairs, a desk or a table, paper and pens for gathering information. Operators who are paid or volunteers have to be recruited, selected, and trained. Someone has to coordinate and supervise the operators, devise work schedules, and in general, "manage" the activity. Some portion of a bookkeeper's time will be required to record and pay bills for services—telephone, rent, supplies, payroll, advertising, and so forth. The question at this point is not "who" does what functions, but "what" functions need to be done to have this activity produce whatever services are intended. The necessary functions could be carried out by one or more people, skilled or unskilled, paid or volunteer. A person responsible for the management functions of a hotline could also be a part-time operator.

Determining resource requirements is partly based on the magnitude of the functions. Is there a full-time job composed of the hiring, supervising, and coordinating the hotline activity? Will this be a 24-hour service? Are two or three phones necessary? The answer to questions about activities design may be known by you or others who are involved in similar activities. Different designs require different functions to be performed and amounts of resources specified. Where new and experimental activities are to be developed, there may be little experience to draw upon to determine the level and kinds of human and material resources required. More unknowns may have to be assumed in order to define the functions that are involved. More "educated" guesswork is involved in planning. In sum, fundamental to translating activities into their financial dimensions is a thoughtful effort of explicitly defining activities in terms of functions and correspondent resources, as is illustrated in Table 1, "Activities, Functions, and Resources."

Table 1 illustrates a possible program design whose goals are prevention and intervention. The three service activities in order of priority are based on what was thought to be most needed and most effective in the community at this time. Overall management and organizational functions to support these services are also shown.

Summary of Program and Budget Planning

Your planning orientation for a project or organization is to clarify as best as you possibly can the general goals and strategy for achieving these goals. Selecting activities will then be a meaningful task. Determine, as best as you possibly can, the resources you will need for program and organizational functions that translate your ideas into action. It is from this planning base that projections of

TABLE 1. Activities, Functions, and Resources: Child Abuse Prevention and Treatment Services

ACTIVITY	FUNCTIONS[a]	PERSONNEL	NON-PERSONNEL
1. Hotline	Publicity Agency liaison Recruiting Training Scheduling Supervising Maintenance of records	Coordinator Operators (paid or volunteer)	Office space Phones Desks/chairs Office supplies

2. PARENTING PROGRAM	Agency liaison
	Publicity
	Organizing/leading
	  groups
	Referral
	Follow-up of clients
	Recordkeeping
	Brochures
		Group therapist
		Part-time secretary
			Office space
			Telephone
			Office supplies
			Office furniture
			Office equipment
			  files
			  typewriter
			Printing

3. PUBLIC AWARENESS
CAMPAIGN (PAC)
	Design and make
	  presentations
	Interagency liaison
	Organize seminars &
	  speakers
	Distribute printed
	  information
		Coordinator
		Assistant
			Travel funds
			Telephone
			Printing and
			  advertising
			Publicity
			Office supplies &
			  equipment

PROGRAM MANAGEMENT	Project coordination Financial management Personnel supervision Publicity Fund raising Reporting Audit Legal services Evaluation	Program coordinator Part-time secretary Bookkeeper Accountant Lawyer	Similar office needs Travel funds Insurance Copy machine

[a]Functions are determined by the particular design of the activity. Given an activity design, personnel requirements can be determined along with nonpersonnel support.

costs of resources can be calculated, and budgets (quantitative plans) developed. Schematically, the process is as follows:

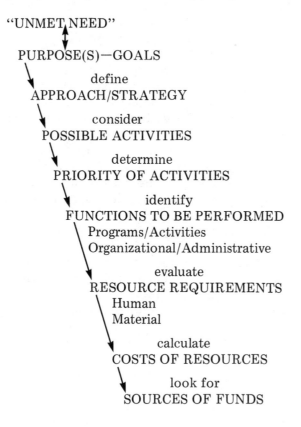

"UNMET NEED"

PURPOSE(S)—GOALS

define
APPROACH/STRATEGY

consider
POSSIBLE ACTIVITIES

determine
PRIORITY OF ACTIVITIES

identify
FUNCTIONS TO BE PERFORMED
Programs/Activities
Organizational/Administrative

evaluate
RESOURCE REQUIREMENTS
Human
Material

calculate
COSTS OF RESOURCES

look for
SOURCES OF FUNDS

OTHER TYPES OF SMALL NONPROFIT ORGANIZATIONS

New and diverse organizations form all the time. The previous example of a human services effort, largely financed by government-sector purchasing, was chosen because it is typical of local organizations that have become a substantial part of the private nonprofit sector in the past two decades. The question of looking at other types of organizations—performing and fine arts, information distribution and media, advocacy and public action, associations of professional groups, common-interest clubs (sports, collectors, alumni), community economic development, church activities, and so on—still require the same approach to planning as applied from responses to the questions asked on page 24. By focusing in on the purposes of the organization, determining the strategy for achieving them, and analyzing clearly the activities to be carried out, you can unveil the mysteries of budget formulation and financial planning. The emphasis of this book on publicly supported (financially) private nonprofit organizations is in response to the growing public awareness of the need for and expanding interest in managing resources used for the public well-being. This is a result of the gradual shift from a charity to "investment" mentality in the public sector. Regardless of the individual *purposes* and *sources* of funding, the overall appreciation for developing a workable budget that reflects the priority and design of activities of an organized effort is the crucial starting point of financial management. This is true whether activities generate profits or funding is private, public, or mixed. Once an activity is defined in a purposeful way, then the question of how to finance it is clearer.

Many organizations draw the bulk of their funding from membership fees and dues. Their activities exist to provide special services that their members cannot obtain elsewhere, or that will mutually sustain and benefit their special "community" (of interests). A regional or city art association may provide inexpensive exhibition facilities, a monthly newsletter about events and services of particular interest to its members, a technical assistance program about the business aspects of being self-employed (bookkeeping, taxes, contracts, marketing), an educational series on artists' techniques, cooperative purchases, and a place to meet. The number of activities that might be of value to the artists/ members (users) are almost limitless, but would be defined and ranked by those trying to fulfill some need(s) of the community. The types and sources of funding, though not limitless, may be quite varied, depending on the activity—for example, membership dues, program fees, advertising revenues, commission on gallery sales, fund-raising parties, and special artistic events. Essentially, most of the different forms of funding are from the members/ users for different services. Insofar as certain activities and functions may be judged by outside (nonmember) funding sources to be of a larger social, professional, and communal benefit, other funds may be available to the organization. For example, some foundations and government agencies may want to support the general purpose of promoting arts or particular educational activities in the area. That support may benefit the members directly or in a limited way, as in the case in which the organization may sponsor summer arts courses for children in the city financed by the local department of education. Thus some activities and events can be paid for directly by the users (members or nonmembers) on a one-time basis. Others, like administrative and office functions, or printing of the newsletter, are regular functions the organization has to provide. In other words, ongoing functions, both administrative and programmatic, that are needed to support the general purpose and existence of the organized effort, require a steady, ongoing funding regardless of whatever other specific programs are planned. "Funding" of essential resources for these functions come from member contributions, public grants and contracts, volunteer services, user fees, sales, or a combination thereof. Assuring that these "shell" functions are financed is the underpinning of any organizational planning and operation. Programmatic activities and events change, and they have different types and sources of funding related to their usefulness and the demand of users.

Consider a local theater company that relies partly on public funding from a local foundation, a few major individual contributors, and the audiences that pay for tickets. The latter source of funding is from specific events—performances. There are costs associated with each specific event as well as the general operation of the theater company. Ticket money may not fully finance a given performance or a group of them; or it may provide more than the cost of the performances. Other sources may be better for the assurance of functions for the general existence of the organization—space, telephone, publicity, general administration, and technical program development (a director). While no one can count on the maximum amount of money the group could generate through performances, an estimate can be made about the minimum amount that is needed to cover the costs of essential resources and functions of the organization.

In summary, the financial planning of resource requirements of all organized efforts can be viewed in a twofold context of (1) necessary organization functions and (2) program activities. In this context you can see that if program activities are significantly expanded, they require more organizational support. The simplest example is the added need for more bookkeeping work. If the person who performs the bookkeeping support functions is essentially fully occupied by current operations, then additional program activities will generate a new requirement of more bookkeeping staff time. That expanded function (and others of administration and coordination) will require financing, either from the sources paying for the new activities or from those supporting the general organizational purposes, or both. The *total* costs of new products or services has to be recognized and regularly accounted for in a financial translation of resource needs and use. The larger and necessary perspective of "financing" means both sources of cash as well as contributions of physical resources, and personal skills.

4

Financial Translation: Costs, Budgets, and Financial Planning

WHAT IS THE "COST" OF A PROJECT?

The resources needed to implement the functions and activities of any organized effort can be translated into costs. As a program director or manager, you are responsible for acquiring and using resources in your organization. Careful identification of functions to be performed means a better analysis of resource specifications and estimates of their costs. The resource elements can be grouped in general categories such as salaries and personnel support, office costs, equipment, or each resource individually listed. No matter how they are presented, generally or specifically, they should come from some type of analysis of activities.

Total project "cost" is a valuation of *all* resources needed to carry out your activities. The strategy design influences the level and types of costs, because it determines the definition of resources. Someone else looking at the same goals may have a different approach to achieving them. Therefore that person's cost estimates would vary from yours, since his or her activities choices would be different. Such is part of the basis of the argument that often goes on between funding sources and organizations that develop and undertake projects.

One criteria for "cost" is reasonableness. Electric typewriters are priced between $250 and $850. What is a "reasonable" cost for this piece of equipment? The answer is better understood if the question is rephrased to ask, "What tasks have to be performed?" Even though you might want a typewriter with all the extras, this may not be necessary or reasonable in terms of project requirements. Reasonableness also means that the lowest possible price of a resource does not necessarily have to be used. You want to be ready to pay "up to" a certain amount for personnel, services, and materials. In the actual purchases, you may be able to negotiate lower prices. The question is, "What is the normal amount necessary to acquire a particular resource?"

Volunteers are sources of funding. Insofar as they are needed to carry out a function of an activity or program, their value should be included as part of the total cost of a project. Many projects depend on volunteers. Hotlines are a good example. Operators perform a critical and often skillful task. Their work has value; it is essential to the activity. How do you place a value on their service? If the same people would have to be paid, what is the wage for the type of work they do?

The U.S. Department of Health and Human Services (HHS) applies three criteria for evaluating the inclusion in project costs of services of volunteers, and "in-kind" (non-cash) contributions:

1. Are they necessary?
2. Do you have control over the resources? (Are they really yours when you need them?)
3. Do they have a clear monetary value?

These criteria are applicable to almost any project where determining total costs of resources is being calculated.

HHS recognizes that regardless of the sources from which the resources are acquired, they have a monetary value to the project if they meet the stated criteria. Look again at the hotline activity. Volunteers contribute their time and skills. Are they worth something? Sure! Are they a real cost of the project? As long as they meet the criteria, the answer is "yes." They perform a needed function. You have control as long as their input is provided on the basis of your scheduling and not their whims. It would be inconsistent to say that their work is necessary to your activity, but you have no control over its utilization! If you had to pay for their skills, can you assign a reasonable value based on a market determination? Minimum wage? Receptionist/telephone operator salary? Mental health assistant?

The point is that *the total cost of the program or project is the monetary value that would be needed to fully pay for all the resource components required to produce the activities.* The sources of funding are irrelevant for project valuation purposes.

HOW TO MAKE COST ESTIMATES

The question is, "What is the normal charge necessary to acquire a particular resource?" While the states and the federal government have plenty of statistics about the average wages of different types of jobs and skills, you have immediate information available. The local newspapers provide a local market basis for the value of different and specific skills in the employment advertisements. Local government agencies set competitive rates for both skills and experience. Other nonprofit organizations near you have to attract and pay competent people. What are their salary levels? New organizations, like new businesses, may not be able to afford competitive salaries, but they offer opportunities of growth and new experiences, as well as the potential of higher salaries in the future.

Professional services, program and management consulting, legal and accounting services are a little more difficult to determine. The main concern is to be clear about what services will be performed. Talk to potential providers about the "problem" to be solved or specific service to be rendered. Get an explanation in writing if possible of what they will do and what it will cost. This information may be used later in a formal offer or bid to supply a resource or service. Legal and accounting services are often charged on an hourly and daily basis. Consultants too often charge by the job or on a daily basis. Seek information from those who have direct experience with what you want done. A lawyer whose main work is business and family practice usually knows little about criminal and juvenile legal procedures. When people are to provide technical services which you cannot do, your organization has to rely upon their performance. Once you have a clear idea of what has to be done, ask for bids from three possible suppliers of services. The same procedures apply to the purchase of any services. If painting and carpentry need to be done, obtain written bids which provide an explanation of the work to be done for a given price. Request for bids from business establishments can be used for the purchase of any large item—a refrigerator, a used truck, a typewriter, plumbing improvements, and the like. In fact, state and federal procurement procedures often require that bids for specific work and goods are solicited before a purchase is made. In that way the funding sources can be assured that you have the best price for what is needed.

Another method for initial estimation for proposal purposes is to use merchandise catalogues of major retailers. They will provide a basis for estimating "reasonable costs" for products available in your area. As mentioned earlier, when the actual purchase is made, it may be for less than originally estimated. Cost estimating is based on projection of a reasonable price. If purchases will be made at a time not in the immediate future, consideration should be given to the possibility of price changes. Think ahead!

HOW COSTS ARE RELATED TO SOURCES

Table 2 is a translation of the functions and resources of the project activities in Table 1 into dollar values shown in the Total Project Cost column. It also shows total cost related to sources of funding for each component. It assumes full-time operation for one year. It shows where resource costs reflect a lesser utilization—i.e., a part-time secretary—and one-time expenditures such as employment advertisements in the newspapers. While Table 1 shows the activities and resource requirements in order of their priority with the administrative part embracing all of the program's administrative needs, the focus of Table 2 is on the difference between the project cost in terms of total resources required and costs in terms of cash required. It relates all the resources used in the project to who will "pay" for them. It helps pinpoint planning deficiencies of certain functions and resources, and highlights financial gaps.

Each resource component is priced in column 1. The sum of these determines the "full cost" of the project. Column 2 is the Organization Budget, representing the dollars needed to pay for resources. In this case, it is from a contract for services to the Department of Mental Health, plus a small amount from the local corporation. Other agents are "financing" different resources, as shown in column 3. Volunteers through their services are financing certain components of the project costs. The used office furniture does have a market value, so a cost can be determined. It is "financed" by the donee.

Most important in your analysis of project and activity funding is a clear focus on needed managerial functions as separate from program activities. Financing the expansion of various man-

	Total Project Cost	Organization Budget[a]	(OTHER SOURCES) Non-Cash	Cash
Personnel				
Program Coordinator	$ 14,000	$14,000		
Secretary/Bookkeeper	8,000	8,000		
Hotline Coordinator	10,000	10,000		
Group Leader,	13,000		Family Center	
part-time assistant	6,000	6,000		
PAC Coordinator	11,000	11,000		
Assistant	9,000	9,000		
Subtotal	$ 71,000	$58,000		
Hotline Volunteers[b]	$ 24,000		Volunteers	
Fringe Benefits (20%)	$ 14,200	$ 9,800	Family Center	
Travel @ 18¢/mi. 200/miles/mo.	$ 432	$ 432		
Non-Personnel				
2 hotline telephones @ $50/mo.	$ 600	$ 600		
Project phone @ $100/mo.	1,200	1,200		
Office Supplies & Postage @ $25/mo.	300	300		
Rent, incl. utilities @ $200/mo.	2,400	1,200	Family Center	
Office Furn. & Eqpt.	1,200		Corporation	
Ad. for Personnel	500	500		
Printing & Publicity	1,000	500	Corporation	
Legal	500		Lawyer	
Insurance	600	600		
Accounting/Auditing	1,200		Corporation	
Total	$118,732	$72,132	$46,600	-0-
Unrestricted		$ 2,900		Corporation

aThis budget, with the exception of the $2,900, is financed under a contract from the DMH. The corporate donation is non-cash and cash for a general use (unrestricted).
bThe value of the volunteers' functions has been roughly determined by minimum wage rates of a 35-hour week for one year, two phones, 14 hours per day, five days per week.

agement functions is often overlooked or undervalued in growing or changing organizations. The result is loss of external credibility and internal controls, which eventually destroys the organization.

It follows that as new projects are planned and added to an existing organization, managerial functions may also have to be expanded. While this is an obvious statement, many organizations enter somewhat blindly into financing arrangements of new proj-

TABLE 3. Organization–Program Structure

ADMINISTRATIVE FUNCTIONS		
Marketing	Production	Finance
Fund raising	Interagency coordination	Financial controls
Publicity	Contract management	Payroll
Proposal development	Technical supervision	Bookkeeping
	Evaluation & planning	Reporting
PROGRAM ACTIVITIES		
A (Parents)	B (Children)	C (Advocacy)
Hotline	Temporary shelter	Research
Parenting groups	Professional services	Conferences
PAC	Special education	

ects that will not provide any or adequate funding for administrative support, but add considerable workload to the organization. Worse, many funding sources naively and arbitrarily refuse to recognize that someone has to pay for the managerial functions necessary to sound operations. Then they wonder why carrying out the agreements they made becomes so difficult. At the least, managers and board members have to realize that projects cannot automatically be added to the organization's activities without an assessment of current availability of managerial resources and the potential need of additional administrative support. The members of the governance board are responsible for the funding of new commitments of the organization. When they consider the budget of a new activity, they have to ask about its effect on the capacity of managerial resources of the organization to absorb those activities. Not to do so is a gross failure on their part, particularly in rapidly growing organizations.

Any organization can have a multitude of activities and funding sources. In fact, a multiproject, multifunded organization could show each different source of financing of individual projects and even activity components. Table 3 illustrates what the overall organizational design might look life if the activities of Table 2 were part of a compilation of several programs in a large organization whose managerial activities embraced the support of additional purposes and activities.

The future evolution of the Child Abuse Project whose budget is shown on Table 2 could look like Table 4, "Multiprogram Budget." Each program and its composite activities would have to

36

TABLE 4. Multiprogram Budget.[a]

		Total Cost	Organization Budget	Sources
ADMINISTRATION				
Personnel		$ 45,000		Family Center
Consultants		4,000		Dept. Mental Health
Office Costs				Dept. Social Services
Phone		1,200		United Way
Rent		3,600		Corporate
—		4,200		
—		2,700		
—	*Subtotal*	$ 60,700	$ 52,900	
PROGRAMS				
I. *Hotline*				
Personnel		$ 34,000		
Non-Personnel		1,200		
	Subtotal	$ 35,200	$ 9,400	
Parenting				
Personnel		$ 25,000		
Non-Personnel				
	Subtotal	$ 25,000	$ 25,000	
PAC				
Personnel		$ 20,000		
Non-Personnel				
	Subtotal	$ 20,000	$ 20,000	
II. *Temporary Shelter*				
Personnel		$ 38,000		
Non-Personnel		12,000		
	Subtotal	$ 50,000	$ 38,600	
Professional Services				
Personnel		$ 30,000		
Consultants		8,000		
Non-Personnel		3,800		
	Subtotal	$ 41,800	$ 41,000	
Special Education		$ 16,000		
	Subtotal	$ 16,000	$ 12,000	
III. *Research Contract*		$ 47,000		
	Subtotal	$ 47,000	$ 45,000	
	Total	$295,700	$243,900	

[a]The budget of Table 2 was the base to which other program and administrative costs were added as the organization grew.

37

be developed in functional detail and resource breakdown in order to develop this budget. Note that administrative functions would probably remain the same in nature, regardless of the number of programs. Each one is essential and characteristic of the overall operation of the organization. As more programs are added and expanded, diverse administrative support efforts are bound to increase. Can they be absorbed or fulfilled with available personnel or not? Can the tasks be reorganized for greater productivity? The problem of cost estimation is based on detailed resource requirements.

A budget picture would probably look like Table 4, Multiprogram Budget," which could be the future evolution of the Program Activities (A). Each program and its composite activities would have to be developed in functional detail. Note that administrative functions would probably remain the same regardless of the number of programs. Each one is essential to the functioning of the organization. The problem of cost estimation is "How much?" As more programs are added or expanded, administrative support functions may require the efforts of a full-time person, or more, for each one.

ORGANIZATION BUDGETING VS. FUNDING-SOURCE OPERATIONS

What is important in *developing* budgets for new programs and making a serious review of expenditures of an ongoing organization is looking at the financial support of functional components of both administrative and program activities. Only by carefully assessing these components can you make reasonable estimates of the costs of resources necessary to produce your activities, services, or products. These resource costs are the raw data for different users and for reporting requirements. This financial information can be arranged in diverse patterns for various purposes of management information, controls, and accounting.

Because funding sources, especially government agencies that are purchasing services, are concerned with their own fiscal controls, the main orientation of their contracting activities is toward "line item" or "objective" budgets. Such budgetary presentations are in the form of gross categories of expenditures—personnel, consultants, office costs, capital costs—or detailed line items of each individual resource cost in a project. These budget formats reflect contractual allocations of their funds for fiscal periods, rather than the operating frameworks of the recipient organizations or projects. Their contracts ask, "What resources in dollar amounts will be needed to produce what we want to buy?" There is no particular reason why funding sources should be overly interested in a managerial or organizational format, since they are basically buying some quantity of products or services for so many dollars. Thus budgeting, as a managerial concern and organizational requirement, should be developed programmatically and functionally and from as many sources as possible. The budgeting format, which is mainly a response to funding-source data and grant conditions, is generally not consistent with the ongoing planning and development of an organized and lasting effort.

"Program budgeting" is organizationally based. It is a way of relating costs to individual program activities and their objectives, in terms of both operations and output. It is a reflection of careful analysis of activities, functions performed, and resource utilization matched with specific objectives. It facilitates clearer thinking about component costs and decisions to allocate funds to specific activities. As an organization grows and changes from a one- or two-activity operation to a larger operation, there is more of a need to look at "what is being done and by whom," changes in organizational structure or the way of doing things, activity priorities, the actual use of available resources, and the output achieved.

The purpose of program budgeting is to focus on how you are in fact employing resources, and weighing priorities in terms of costs and output. In an ongoing organization, an important job at the highest managerial level is to fully understand what the scope of activities is and what their actual costs are. Many resource uses can be allocated in some way to various activities: rent, telephone, office costs, and the like. How does the executive director actually spend his or her time? In terms of organization objectives, how should this person be employed—interagency coordination, proposal development, financial management, bookkeeping, typing letters? Each of these functions requires different skills that have a wide range of market values. For what functions and output is your organization really paying each of its employees? How do the staff members in your organization actually spend their time?

Each functional breakdown is subject to one or more activity allocations. Thus an activity can be "costed." The cost components provide a basis for estimating the costs of new activities, reconsideration of priorities, and allocation of resources.

BUDGET CHANGES AND
FUNDING-SOURCE RESTRICTIONS

The financial management terminology of "restricted" and "unrestricted" funds or funding refers to an agreement, implicit or explicit, on the part of your organization and the funding source(s) about the use of its/their funds. Insofar as funds that your organization has or will receive are destined by contract or grant for a specific program or function, they are "restricted." For instance, if you have a contract with a government agency to carry out a service project such as the one in our example, funds from that agency are to be used in accordance with an agreed-upon budget for specific activities. Through detailed budgets, accounting procedures, and reimbursement control, funding sources are often able to enforce these contracts.

"Unrestricted" funds are monies that are not limited to a specific use by their source. Such funds may come from fund drives, fees, donations, bequests, or grants that provide for "general support" of your program goals. "Unrestricted" implies that your organization and its representatives have not made any conditions or promises about specific use when acquiring the funds. If you represent that you are seeking money for capital purchases—a residence, equipment, renovation, a vehicle, or the like—and a source provides these funds, then most likely a "restriction" has been assumed about the use for these things by the donor or grantor. Spending such funds to meet deficits already incurred for other purchases would be breaking the agreement.

Sometimes the restrictions are broad, leaving specific decisions to the organization. It is not uncommon that a source will fund "operating expenses"—office expenses, salaries, and so forth. The concept of restrictedness has to do with a contractual relationship. The funding party wants to maintain a degree of control over decisions to make purchases of resources by the recipient organization. It wants to be assured that money is spent according to mutually agreed-upon purposes. Control inevitably refocuses on accountability to the funding source. Usually the less control, the fewer the demands and concerns about specific use. The general purpose of the organization is supported when unrestricted funding is used. Nevertheless, while certain funds may have minor or no restrictions, the board of directors, officers, or those responsible for the activities of the project or organization are still accountable for how these funds are in fact spent. Their guideline is the stated purpose of the organization and the priorities for activities to be undertaken. Thus all funds are "restricted" in an organizational sense, if not a contractual one. The fundamental question of use and priorities is "How will this expenditure advance the achievement of our goals?"

YOU *MUST* PLAN FOR FINANCIAL FLEXIBILITY

As a practical matter, any plan for financing your activities requires a little "extra" for the unknown conditions of the future. Unrestricted funds provide the managerial flexibility to meet and respond to the changing financial and resource requirements of implementation. The appearance of unforeseen costs and functions, or required changes in activities' design, or the implementation strategy are almost inevitable. Unrestricted funds can be seen as reserves for underestimates of cost. They can also support complementary projects of research training, consulting, experimental or pilot (test) activities, and other functions sometimes discovered to be necessary to realize, enlarge, or revise expectations about a previous action framework. By referring to program priorities, unrestricted funds can be allocated in accordance with some organizational guidelines.

Managers sometimes find they are "locked into" a budget or contract. They seek ways to "juggle" the funds or do "creative bookkeeping" to give them so-called financial flexibility. Indeed, they are "locked into" making expenditures according to the agreements that have been developed with their funding sources. If the activities and functions were poorly defined in the first place, financial manipulations are not the answer.

But even well-developed budgets are projections of the costs of future activities. They are rarely viewed as carved in stone. The financial shortcomings arise because budget expectations clash with reality of actual costs and revenue flow. Amendments, mutually agreed-upon contract modifications, recognize that previous agreements may have to be altered as financial or other problems arise in project implementation. Amendments usually require mutual agreement in writing and by authorized persons. To change a budget allocation of a project in a significant way without consent of the funding source is to negate a funding agreement and sometimes change the mutually agreed-upon plan of activities. When an agreement with the funding source is broken by your organization, the former is no longer obligated to provide funds to your organization or fund "unauthorized" expenditures. The funding source often has legal rights to recover funds not used in accordance with agreements you have made. Other alternatives to trying to change the agreements are raising additional unrestricted funds, or adding complementary projects that may finance certain costs of the ongoing project.

The newer and more original a project, the more financial flexibility there has to be to acquire and manage resources and individuals. Less is known about costs and outcome of planning of such projects. Thus to support planning and implementation, some form of unrestricted funds is usually needed by the organization. Financial flexibility is an organizational requirement. It is not a derivative of arbitrary decisions on the part of officers or the financial manager to reallocate funds. It is part of overall financial planning strategy, and the seeking of particular types of financing, as we see in Figure 2.

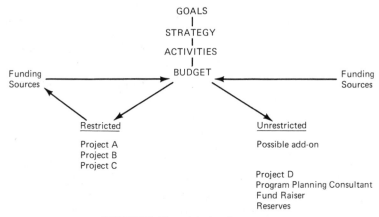

FIGURE 2. Financial planning strategy.

ADMINISTRATIVE EFFICIENCY: INDIRECT/DIRECT COSTS

At one point or another, everyone is concerned about administrative costs necessary to support a service, program, or product. How much of a dollar spent actually goes directly into service activity of the project rather than to the administrative functions? Stating the question in management terms, "What is the minimum amount of expenses necessary for the managerial support of the specific service(s)?" Let's look at organizations with which we are familiar to gain a broader perspective before discussing the financial management concepts and calculations.

The Boy Scouts, the Heart Fund, the YMCA, and other local and national organizations are constantly raising public funds for their programs. As a contributor, you may want to be assured that most of the money you give them goes directly into their services, rather than to administrative salaries and office expenses. Put yourself in the position of being the administrator of the local "Y." It is budget preparation time. You feel you need to hire an assistant, rather than start a new program. You see yourself as understaffed and overworked, a not uncommon complaint of any manager of a small human service organization. This assistant would make your job a little easier, but more important, would free up some time for you to evaluate the current programs and to help develop new ones.

Now let's suppose you were a member of the board of directors of this same "Y." You and other members are reviewing the proposed budget for the following year. In this role, one of your concerns might be that the largest part of the budget be used for activities of the "Y," such as more summer programs, year-round teenage sports, and the like. You are a person who is responsive to concerns of some local contributors and community residents who believe that too much money may be "wasted" on administrative salaries. However, since you are also knowledgeable about organizational change, you want to weigh the overall managerial needs of the future against the current program needs before you vote on the budget for the following year.

Switch roles again; you are a staff member. You want a raise in salary, just to keep up with inflation, and you would also like to have a merit raise that recognizes your productivity. Your job now encompasses much more responsibility than a year ago when you started. You have developed an innovative program concept that will expand your career potential, if the "Y" supports it. The director thinks it would be successful in reaching a large number of teenagers. However, a new staff member would have to be hired to help you carry out the activities. The project would have to be approved as a new activity in the new budget by the board of directors.

These viewpoints all reflect the differing interests and claims to budget allocations in terms of what are called "direct" (program) and "indirect" (administrative) costs. Arguments between "program" people and administrators often revolve around allocating funds between organization functions and program activities. There are no easy answers for deciding what allocations are needed or desirable at a given time in a growing or changing organization. But appreciating that the administrative resource needs of the organization change as programs expand (and contract) helps focus any discussion on allocation of funds.

In a growing organization, the question of administrative capacity is translated to "What organizational functions have to be added or expanded in order to provide new services or support (near) future program objectives?" For example, an accounting system may have to become more detailed and embrace new procedures. It may increase in cost per se, but relative to the total current and anticipated expenditures, it may be a declining percent of the total budget. The increase is needed to produce information required to have better records of expenditures, and to provide reports to management and funding sources. Some administrative functions might be easier as a result, and additional programs could be added with only a minor increase of costs to the accounting system. Efficiency in this case would be derived from spending more money on accounting functions at this point in the development of the organization.

Another example is the common condition of an organization manager carrying out most of the bookkeeping tasks. The board claims that there is not enough money to hire a bookkeeper, and they are worried about controls. But in fact they are often paying a manager at a higher salary to perform a less costly administrative skill. As a result, the administrative functions that have higher cost and value—coordination, planning, proposal development, grantsmanship—are not being done. Additional investment in the bookkeeping function, even by the treasurer, would free up the time of the administrator to expand the programs to in fact pay for a part- or full-time person for the bookkeeping work.

Though administrative capacity of an operation is an important managerial and financial concept, there are no formulas for easy analysis, especially for small and rapidly growing organizations. Only by a regular evaluation of the administrative functions necessary to carry out contractual requirements, programmatic objectives, and longer-range goals can the adequacy of an administrative budget be determined. No two operations are alike. Wages, rents, insurance, and other costs vary in different locations. The types, quantity, and quality of services or activities that are produced also vary. Even organizations carrying out the same project—a hotline—may have different operating designs, thereby requiring different resource inputs. Furthermore, every organization and program are in different stages of implementation—start-up, consolidation, expansion, and so forth. The extent of administrative support functions varies with each of these stages. Initial implementation of activities usually requires concentrated administrative effort. Nevertheless, as a member of a governance structure or as a manager, it is important for you to see that administrative costs are spread as "thin" but sufficiently as possible in support of program activities. However, administrative costs must be future-oriented. As much as possible, they should include expenditures for resources that do not necessarily produce immediate results, such as financial and program consultants, or training, planning, and fund-raising functions. To have low administrative costs does not mean excluding expenditures for resources that are used for tomorrow's organizational efforts.

"RATES": FUNDING-SOURCE VIEWS OF COSTS

In the Public Health Service's *Grants Policy Statement*, the Department of Health and Human Services defines indirect costs as "the costs incurred by an organization that is not readily identifiable with a particular project or program but is nevertheless necessary to the operation of the organization and the performance of its programs." Graphically, the costs that appear in Table 2 can be separated as shown in Figure 3.

In theory, all administrative costs could be charged to a particular project or program. Look again at Table 1, Chapter 3. All those functions listed under "Program Management" are for the purpose of supporting the activities of the organization. Each service activity bears a portion of the costs of these essential administrative functions. But how do you divide the general telephone costs among the three services? How are the salaries of

FIGURE 3. Costs division.

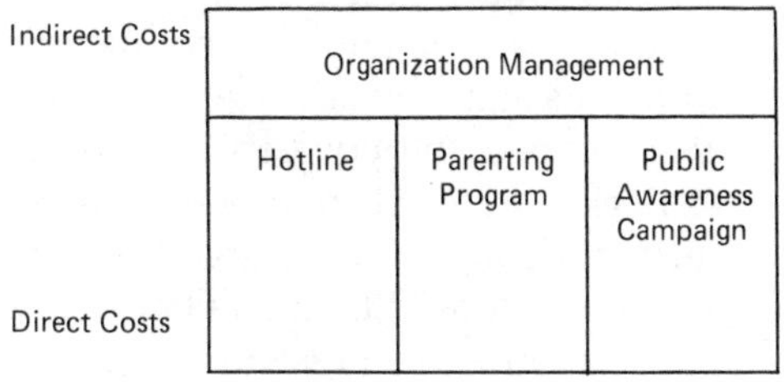

Indirect Costs	Organization Management		
	Hotline	Parenting Program	Public Awareness Campaign
Direct Costs			

the secretary and the coordinator divided among the three services? The rent is probably an easier calculation. Each service occupies a certain amount of space which can be separated from the administrative space. But then there is still a matter of dividing the costs of administrator's office and conference room among the services! Should these be divided (1) equally among the program activities, (2) proportionate to dollar or personnel size of activities, or (3) on a time/utilization basis? Can they be reasonably apportioned or allocated by any of these methods?

It would be wonderfully convenient if, after putting together the budget (the costs that were specifically identifiable) for a new project or significant activity, you could use some formula to add on the difficult-to-determine administrative costs. But as noted earlier, these vary in accordance with functions and existent managerial structure. Their compilation may require serious thought about organizational changes and the complexity of managing new program ventures.

Some funding sources have established pre-set cost formulas that are basically their funding limitations. Certain projects funded by HHS in the areas of training and research have fixed an 8 percent indirect-cost limit. Many state agencies apply a limit on specific types of projects. The limit may or may not have any relationship to your organizational requirements. One formula used in Massachusetts by the Department of Mental Health for certain projects is: 10 percent of salaries or 8 percent of project costs, exclusive of donated or in-kind resources. In calculating the direct program costs, administrative costs such as secretarial and other management functions of the activity could be included as identifiable costs. In applying this formula to the Child Abuse Program, think of the latter as a complete new project for the Family Counseling Center. The Center would propose this program to the Department of Mental Health and request an additional "administrative overhead" of 10 percent of salaries or 8 percent of the "program" budget. A contract would generally indicate what administrative functions are expected for this rate. This overhead would be used for indirect costs of management incurred by the Family Counseling Center as a result of implementing the project. Those costs of added accounting functions, supervision, contract coordination and management, liaison work, and so forth would, it is hoped, be covered by this formula. However, no manager, officer, or board member should assume that such formulas will automatically cover costs. A functional analysis of the added indirect costs should be made before a proposal is submitted.

Where cost rates are not previously established, many funding sources calculate a level of funding for managerial costs of a new project based upon the ongoing costs of the organization. The determination of that level of "indirect cost rate" by a funding source requires calculation of only those costs which the funding source allows.

HHS will not allow costs of bad debts, entertainment, interest, and except under very special circumstances, pre-award expenses in the indirect-rate calculation. Each federal, state, or local agency that utilizes some type of rate setting will have its own basis for allowability of cost elements. Grants Policy Statement of HHS offers a useful and probably much-copied guideline. Different funding sources have their own way of calculating such rates. The end result is the same—an indirect-cost rate is tailored to your organization's cost structure. Once you are given a rate by a funding source, it may be applicable to future projects funded by that same source. However, changes in organizational activities and managerial costs, reflected in the annual financial statements, have to be reviewed and recalculated. Thus rates are usually modified on an annual basis.

Assume that the Child Abuse Program was in full operation and funds were sought for a new program, a temporary shelter. A funding source is considering the new proposal and is reviewing the financial information to determine an indirect cost rate for the organization.

Figure 4 shows a graphic presentation of the different aspects of the concept of direct and indirect costs.

There are various accounting and other problems concerning

FIGURE 4. Child abuse services.

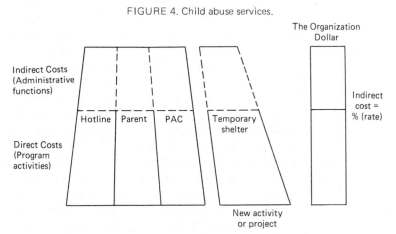

Total cost of the new project = rate times the direct costs + the direct costs

the concepts and practices of determining indirect-cost rates. The most important and most relevant for purposes of this book has to do with communication. You cannot assume, when such labels as "administrative" costs, "overhead," "support" costs, and so forth are used, that everyone understands what they mean or that in fact the same definitions are shared. Thus, if you keep in mind the functional nature of "total" costs (including contributed resources) of organizational management and program activities, you will be able to ask understandable questions about rate-setting policies and calculations.

THE MAGIC OF A 90-DAY BUDGET

Thus far, budgets have been discussed within a static framework. The budget illustrated in Table 2 of a one-year projection is a "picture" of costs which assumes *full* operation of proposed activities. If your funding agents or an astute member of the board of this organization were to ask what will be done in the first 90 days of the project, you would realize that this budget does not indicate a spending guide or plan of action to arrive at full operation. Most of us think in terms of complete projects and the component resources necessary to produce them. However, a plan for the acquisition of resources and their financing requirements can and should be developed for each project. Such a plan describes a flow of organizing decisions about when different resources will be purchased for starting different functions and activities. For example, setting up the hotline at the Child Abuse Center requires advertising for, screening, and hiring of paid personnel; recruitment and training of volunteers; scheduling and supervision of operators; and working out procedures with referral agencies. While the telephone for the Center might be installed immediately, the installation of the hotline telephones would most likely await the training and availability of the volunteer answering staff.

Just in the matter of hiring, many jobs in nonprofit agencies must be publicly advertised because public funds are involved. Writing and placing an advertisement, screening replies, contacting and interviewing, and final selection take time. You may be able to use someone else's space and facilities to get started, but you will have to obtain permanent office space, and order office equipment and furniture. If licenses are required or building codes (fire, safety, handicapped access, and so forth) have to be met before you can proceed with full operations, your "start-up" plan and budget should reflect the time required for obtaining them. The experience of others will often be useful for planning your first steps. People who run hotlines may be able to tell you about the problems of getting them started and continuing them.

While a 90-day period is somewhat arbitrary, the start-up focus is essential to organizing efforts, assigning management responsibilities, measuring results, and planning needed funding to facilitate taking action. When you think carefully about a start-up plan, or close-down (that does happen) plan, you detail many of the actions necessary to give organizational life and order to project activities. You will also make clearer the possible obstacles to full implementation that have to be resolved or overcome in some way. Financial flows and projections can then be derived for a budget. Subsequent program implementation or lack of it will be reflected in a record of actual expenditures.

In Table 1, the functions of each activity were defined to decide what resources would be needed for full operation. With a start-up focus, you consider a step-by-step scheduling of the utilization of these resources. While you may have a concept of the fully operating hotline, you have to start with an available phone, address, and advertisement for staff to operate it. People have to be contacted and interviewed. Someone will be selected as a coordinator, and given certain organizing responsibilities. A plan of management duties and interagency referral arrangements for the hotline have to be developed. Volunteers then have to be recruited, trained, and scheduled. Phones have to be installed and then ongoing operations supervised. Many of these actions translate into expenditures. These expenditures are financial "markers" for project implementation in that they show when resources are expected to be acquired and in use, as the following table illustrates.

Hotline Activity

IMPLEMENTING TASKS					
→ Personnel recruitment	→ Hire	→ Plan operation/ liaison	→ Volunteer recruitment	→ Train/ Schedule	→ Set Up/ Begin

EXPENDITURES (BUDGET ITEMS)				
Advertising	Salaries	Travel Telephone	Advertising	Office Supplies
	Fringe	Office Supplies		Office Furniture
		Secretarial Time		Telephone

What do you project the time span will be to carry out this elementary start-up schedule? A start-up or operational budget with a given time period, whether it is 60, 90, or 120 days, is the projected expenditure based on a plan to start functions and activities. As with all projections, this is what you hope will be the progress of implementing the services. Figure 5, "Start-Up Plan and Bud-

FIGURE 5. A 90-day start-up plan and budget.

	0	1/2	1	1/2	2	1/2	3

OBJECTIVES

Advertise for personnel Hire coordinator	Organize office Hire Secretary Hotline Coord. PAC Coord. Recruit volunteers Set up bookkeeping system Start liaison work	Full staffing and volunteers Start-up of hotline Prepare public relations program

FUNCTIONS

$1,166/m

Coordinator hired —————————————

Advertising

Secretary hired 667/m
Hotline hired 833/m
PAC-C hired 917/m
PAC Asst.

Advertising

Group leader hired 500/m
Asst. hired PR
Volunteers start trng start hotline

Assumptions
— Assistance from Advisory Committee
— Use of space/phones in the family counseling center during the first month
— Personnel hired at budgeted salaries
— Advertising was done for hiring the coordinator

BUDGET

				1166 500 625 459	1166 667 833 250 519		
Personnel	X		875		2750		4352
Fringe 20%	X		175		550		870
Phones:	subtotal		1050		3300		5222
Office				X	35		40
Hotline						X	32
Rent			X		100		100
Office Supplies			X		45		40
Advertising	X	X	300 X		160		
Travel			X		8		20
Insurance						X	600
TOTAL			1350		3648		6054

get," is a translation of the total program into an operational perspective. It shows a budget as a derivative of an organizing plan, rather than a fully operative program. This budget indicates the amount of funding that is expected to be necessary to start your organization.

AN OVERVIEW OF BUDGET PLANNING

Budgets are what you expect will be the expenditures to acquire resources during a specific period of time to implement organizational plans. They are sometimes a matter of educated guesswork about quantities of future costs and when they will occur. Through the application of the concept of start-up or operational budgeting, managerial attention is shifted from conceptualization of a fully operating project of some future time period to the practical business of getting organized. Once you start asking, "How do we get there?" after you have determined "where" you are trying to go and "what" you want to do, the idea of management functions is not so theoretical, nor is the function of management "planning."

Recasting functions and resource acquisition into a time framework highlights the budget problems of predictability and projection. The vulnerability of financial plans generally revolve around the following:

1. The newer or more innovative the activities in a program concept, the less experience there is to draw upon to determine the flow of functions, possible implementation obstacles, and necessary resources.
2. The extent of control that your organization has over decisions affecting the utilization of resources for your programs significantly influences your ability to implement programs and financial plans according to your design. Important external factors abound—interagency agreement, joint programming, conditional funding, licensing, contractual waivers, and the like.
3. The longer the time to reach full operation, the greater the inability to prepare reasonably detailed plans and a time framework for your actions.

Discouraged? You shouldn't be! It is not the perfect plan that counts; what is critical is the focus on organizing (and sharing) the next steps by trying to determine the managerial needs, action, and coordination.

You can and should plan for less-than-ideal situations. In the experience of implementing the start-up plan, variations from the projected time framework, costs of resources, and the start of anticipated functions themselves will usually occur as decisions are carried out. The unexpected will surely happen, regardless of how carefully you have drawn up your plans of action, resource requirements, and financial estimates. Some kind of financial reserve for such contingencies is an important part of any financial plan. It reflects an appreciation of and flexibility about dealing with uncertainty. The flow of implementation of functions is not entirely predictable, nor are the influences of outside factors that are essential to the development of any program or enterprise. The reason many projects get into trouble is that they are not designed with enough of an understanding that what is projected and what will happen are rarely the same.

Most funding sources do not expect perfection. Those that are especially concerned about the planning and implementation of a project usually want to see that you can make reasonable translation of your ideas into some type of action. More important than picturing an ideal outcome is your own shift of orientation to what has to be done to achieve it.

Given this discussion on "planning" (short-range) and the material of the section on the 90-day budget, you should revise the first annual budget shown in Table 2 to adjust for the start-up schedule of the first three months. Such a budget is your organizing and financial map, regardless of whether it is required in part or in full by funding sources.

The next chapters explore the relationship of the projected activities and the organizational functions with the actual expenditures as they are implemented, in terms of management procedures and controls. What you and others plan to do and what you actually spend on doing it are essential components of financial management.

WHAT THE BUDGET MEANS

In its simplest expression, a budget is the estimated cost of a resource acquisition list and expected revenues for a period of time. Viewed as such, it is no more than a document of control (Table 2). It is of little value in organizing diverse talents and efforts of different people, even though it may represent some expression of goals. But a budget seen in the dynamic sense of organizational functions, growth, and guidance provides the following:

For the board of governance—

- A translation of the goals and program objectives into operational schedules and financial boundaries
- A basis for program status and management performance review
- A considered allocation of limited resources at any given time to a set of organizational priorities

For the managers—

- An activities development and priorities plan
- An administrative guideline for day-to-day financial decisions
- A cash-needs projection
- A basis for financial reporting and review of resources utilization, and standard of measurement of the inflow to pay for them

For both, it is the link between the purpose and the action of the organization. The budget is a plan for and a measure of the use of resources for which both interests have their respective accountability.

MANAGERIAL OPERATIONS AND ISSUES

5

The Financial
Management Role

In many small human service organizations, the annual budget is often the budget of a single activity, with most of the funds derived from one or two sources. Consequently, the use of the funds is usually restricted solely to carrying out that project in accordance with a specific funding agreement. The budget, is probably written in extensive detail, with each resource cost a "line item." In other situations, spending may be guided by general program objectives not specifically tied to requirements of a given funding source or sources, as with public-awareness organizations that rely on general-purpose donations such as efforts to save the whales or to provide information about nuclear power. Or a budget may be expressed in broad categories of office expenses, equipment, and personnel. Regardless of its appearance, either you or someone else initially made some calculations about what resources were needed and what they would cost, given a formal or even informal plan of activities.

A budget approval procedure is an explicit allocation of

financial resources to activities by those responsible for the organization. It is, in effect, the creation of a financial map for those who are involved in financing and those purchasing resources for the organization's activities. It is a formal recognition of the financial obligations that are perceived to be necessary to implement the planned activities. It takes into account expected flows of funds into an organization. It is an organizational plan to spend money in a particular way (strategy and priorities) to achieve specific project objectives and organizational goals. As an agreement between various parties—legally or self-appointed "trustees," advisors, community or group representatives, funding sources, and so on—it represents a consensus about what is to be done with finances that the organization has, can, or will obtain. It provides explicit directions, as well as limitations on making purchasing decisions. The approved budget may have to be altered, and even changed substantially because of new information or unforeseen resource needs revealed during program implementation. Nevertheless, it is the mutually agreed-upon starting point.

Whether the overall decision making (governance) is viewed as a collective or hierarchical activity, formal approval of a budget by those who legally or by self-designation have ultimate responsibility for money that is not their own represents an agreement on *how much* an organization will spend to acquire and use resources. The delegation of implementing authority is an internal agreement about *who* will carry out certain decision-making functions on a daily basis. Though the phrase "delegation of authority" sounds weighty and bureaucratically formal, it is simply a focus on giving structure to and defining the limits of implementing decisions within an organized or organizing group of people. It helps avoid confusion and promotes clarity of roles for people working together for a common purpose.

Formal statements of decision-making functions are often incorporated in bylaws of organizations. Such delegations have a dual nature. If a person (administrator or project director) is delegated to act for or make decisions in the name of an organization, he or she is, or should be, responsible to those who empowered the person or supervised the duties for whatever actions were taken. However, in order for a staff person to effectively use and be responsible for the power of using organizational resources (money, equipment, staff time, and so forth), expectations about what a person in a certain role is to do need to be incorporated in the form of plans and expenditures. The budget is the financial guideline for implementing decisions. The more carefully it is developed, the clearer are the directions for spending at all levels

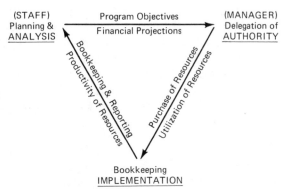

FIGURE 6. Governance/management overview.

of activities. By requiring at the governance level organizational approval of financial plans and delegating authority to people in certain roles, the implementation becomes much more clearly defined and the chance of arbitrary decisions being made is decreased. Any chain of delegation has its correspondent chain of responsibility back to its source. To borrow a financial term, let us refer to the word "accountability"—to account for—instead of the overused word "responsibility." Without an approved budget there cannot be impersonal authorizing decisions, financial direction, or accountability of individuals acting in the name of an organized effort. Figure 6, "The Governance/Management Overview," illustrates the connection between planning, organizational approval, implementation, and "accounting for."

TAKING ON A MANAGER'S PERSPECTIVE

Many valuable ideas fail after being funded because of the inability of the administrator or project manager, as well as board members or advisory and funding groups, to understand and support the financial management requirements needed to achieve their program aims. Budgets and financial plans too often are narrowly perceived as money matters which are in some way a less important part of the "real" work of the organization or as an integral part of the organizing effort per se.

Being an effective organizer or manager in a small operation has a lot to do with shifting from a promotional orientation of attracting the interest and resources of others to a managerial perspective of implementation of plans; from convincing outsiders to support a cause to organizing personnel and activities; and from conceptualization of sound objectives to making the nitty-gritty daily decisions to achieve them. Project costs are no longer abstractions. The program and financial planning was only the beginning. When obligations for purchases are being made and funds start to flow into the checking account, internal organization of and control over expenditures is the emphasis of financial management.

GETTING STARTED

To convey this sense of changing managerial functions from planning to implementation, let's look at the progress of the model proposal.

The town council has accepted your proposal for a child abuse project. The Family Mental Health Clinic and other organizations give strong support to your approaches to reaching and reducing the incidence of abused children. The final shape of the program, after you have spent many hours negotiating, is that it will be independent of the Mental Health Clinic, but will work closely with it. In fact, the Clinic will provide some of the budgeted components of your activities with funding from the city. There will be a separate board of directors, plus an advisory group composed of various representatives of local human service agencies. The most exciting news is that because of your persuasiveness, professional understanding, and enthusiam, you were considered the best candidate to organize the program. As you settle back with feelings of accomplishment, you suddenly realize that the board members will expect you to manage purchases, hire and supervise staff, see that local suppliers are paid, reconcile the checkbook, and present reports on activities and finances of this new program. Of course, you are also responsible for the extensive liaison work with all kinds of agencies and people. The funding commitments are only for one year, even though there are various assurances that financial support of the program will be continued in the following year.

You are hired to work in a newly formed organization and begin to take the responsibilities as its manager. In many organizations these duties are defined in general terms by an organizing group or a board of directors. Where organizations are legally constituted, the board members and officers are responsible for the activities and use of funds. But regardless of organizational forms —traditional hierarchy; collective; with or without an advisory group, board of directors, trustees, or community representatives —financial management procedures and perspectives are essential to the programmatic success, because they will provide information about implementation, a basis for control, and accountability of those persons delegated to make spending decisions. Where do you begin?

MANAGING EXPENDITURES: WHAT'S INVOLVED?

In the overview of financial management, you are concerned with three essential and integrated functions: (1) purchasing resources in accordance with a budget, (2) paying bills and recordkeeping, and (3) financial reporting. These elements are the legs of an organized effort that support the implementation of any plan of action.

THE PURCHASING PROCESS

In a very small project or program, to make expenditures you would take your checkbook or some cash, go to the store, and say, "I want some pads of paper, and some erasers and pencils." The storekeeper would reply, "Here are different kinds—what do you need?" You'd make your selection, check the bill for errors in addition, pay for the items, and take them away with a cash register receipt or an itemized bill. As your program grows, more and more people are involved in an ever-increasing number of similar transactions. Your skills are needed elsewhere. The steps that you may have mechanically performed in the past need to be delegated and systematized to create a reliable purchasing procedure. What were those steps? Initially, you referred to the budget as a guide to purchases. Then you

- Checked to see if you had enough money
- Provided a set of specifications
- Made an offer to buy
- Verified the specs and accepted goods or services
- Checked and paid the bill
- Kept the receipt

In a conventionally structured organization, the board of directors delegates authority to the administrator to make purchases in the name of the organization. This delegation is necessary in order that the day-to-day purchasing activity of program implementation can be carried out. The delegation of this authority sometimes has (or should have) a financial limitation to assure control over major purchases. For example, decisions involving more than $500 might require a review or specific approval of the treasurer of the organization or the full board. It makes sense that large financial commitments are reviewed and specifically approved by the board members. Not only the fact that the board is ultimately financially responsible, but as a practical matter, decisions to undertake significant financial obligations should not be made by any one person in an organization, regardless of his or her competency.

What is important here is that there is an organizational starting point from which authority to spend originates. That authorization can just as easily come from a legal body of officers and directors or from a decision-making body of any kind, a group set up and responsible for that function. That authorizing capability can be defined and redefined in accordance with changing financial or organizational needs. Thus a line of accountability for day-to-day decisions can be flexibly established. Without the line of accountability, the financial decision making may be separated from the organizational purpose. As a consequence, control over the spending process is lost.

In making purchases, the administrator, or the project, business, or financial manager of an organization, is guided by an approved budget. Sometimes he or she will use a "purchase order," a formal offer to a vendor to buy a certain item at a specific price. When the vendor fulfills the request according to specification, a contract between buyer and seller has been completed, and an obligation to pay has been created. With or without a formal offer, an obligation is created when an authorized buyer receives goods and services in response to a specific request.

A "purchase order system" is a method for centralizing authorization in larger organizations, consolidating orders, and unifying budgetary control over expenditures. The decision making about purchases is first generated by a request from whoever needs something to carry out his or her job. This is presented in writing to the person in charge of the purchase order system. That person will check with the budget to see if money is available. The purchase order is a financial control tool, not a program control. Programmatic consideration of expenditures must be made by those in charge of the function or activity—project manager, office manager, supervisor, or chief administrator. All orders are formally presented to suppliers on a purchase order form, which constitutes an offer to buy a resource. Each order is numbered so there is an internal reference against which delivery receipts and suppliers' bills can be matched. Thus the system provides not only an authorization structure but also an important and consistent recordkeeping system for the bookkeeper and accountant. While a purchase order system provides important controls and records, it must be considered in an operational context. Managers are still responsible for screening requests, approving the applicability (programmatic) of a decision, and knowing what is available for their activities. Thus they require regular expenditure reports which tell them how much is still available from their budgets.

Part of the job responsibility and concern of the person in the role of the financial manager is to assure that the financial obligations incurred do, in fact represent the resources the organization was supposed to be buying, and that purchases are within the limits of the approved budget. If each of the purchasing tasks mentioned earlier is carried out, then verification of expenditures is reasonably assured. A common example in a small organization would be found in the practice of the administrator delegating to a secretary the authority and responsibility of ordering and maintaining office supplies. The secretary sees that supplies are needed, places an order, receives and checks what has been delivered, signs a delivery receipt that verifies the delivery (or notes that it was not the same as the order), and keeps a copy of the receipt. If the secretary is also the bookkeeper, then the receipt is filed. If not, it goes to the bookkeeper. It is an informal financial obligation at this point. The supplier sends a bill to the organization based upon what was ordered, but as confirmed by a copy of the signed delivery receipt. The secretary or bookkeeper compares the copy of the signed receipt with the bill. If they do not match, then the vendor should be notified as soon as possible. Sometimes the delivery receipt is the only notice of money owed to the supplier. Then it is the formal billing. The administrator checks the final bill (or receipt/bill) to see that it is consistent with the budgeted amounts and to see how the delegation of the purchasing authority is being carried out. The administrator OKs the bill in his or her role as authorizing agent of the organization. The bill is then ready for payment. Figure 6, Governance/Management Overview," shows management control and documentation of the purchasing procedures in context with other major financial management functions.

The same authorization/specification/validation tasks found on page 61 at the opening of this section comprise the purchasing procedures, regardless of size of an organization or the division of responsibility among staff and others. No tasks should be bureaucratic. Their purposes are to provide financial control in an organized effort. Whether or not there is a formal purchase order system or a less formal approval procedure, the financial management concerns remain the same—budget availability, authorized requests, and validated purchases. As individuals, most of us follow similar, and almost automatic, steps when purchasing goods and services for ourselves. We carry out financial management functions in our own decision about purchases.

THE PERSONNEL CONTRACT: ANOTHER PART OF THE PURCHASING PROCESS

The purchasing process may be very subtle, as in the payment of wages. Each time a paycheck is issued, there has been tacit approval that so many hours of work have been performed, that those hours of skills were the ones contracted for (job description), and that the work was carried out at a certain level of competency. Some organizations have explicit mechanisms in the form of time sheets which administrators and project directors approve before paychecks are issued. Clearly, a signature is more than a mechanical act! It is a verification and an approval to make payment. The procedure of warning an employee that his or her work is not acceptable is essentially a notification to a vendor that the product of an employment contract is not up to specification.

Because personnel are often a significant part of the budget of a private nonprofit organization, especially those in the human services field, some further discussion of this resource element is warranted. Employees, staff, co-workers—all are "suppliers" of skills. Their skills can be highly specialized, as in medical services, or more general, as in secretarial and clerical services. The degree to which each person's skills are refined and productive varies with the person's experience and the organization. The market values of these differences are often reflected in salary ranges. Though employees should be hired in the same way other resources are acquired, those doing the "purchasing" are often unaware that it is the same process.

A skills package designed to fulfill some organizational function(s) is a job description. As shown earlier, it can be derived from a functional analysis of proposed activities and implementation plans. The job description is, in essence, equivalent to the specifications that you would give any supplier of a product or a service that will be needed in the production of an organization's activities. "Screening" of applicants for a position is making a determination of whether or not the supplier's offer of talents and skills fits the resource description and can produce the special functions. For example, you might look for an executive director with certain skills and program experience, whose orientation might be starting up new projects or grants development, or for strengthening the overall operations of an established program. The skills orientation will depend on the organizational needs at a particular time.

An implied or explicit contract is made when an organization accepts a future employee's credentials and he or she begins work. But what often happens is that little or nothing is put in writing. Job descriptions are either perfunctory, mechanical, or left unclear. More important, in rapidly growing organizations, employees are expected to assume new functions and learn new skills. The initial formal or informal agreement does not provide for what becomes a constantly changing contractual relationship.

A contract is a mutual agreement about expectations. When you hire a new person, you ideally consider his or her "best qualities" to fulfill expectations of certain job performance. An employment agreement is a purchase of skills that you hope will match the needed functions of the organization. The supplier/ employee expects certain pay and working conditions, and some minimal idea of the services that will be exchanged. If you think about the acquisition of human resources, you realize this is a highly refined purchasing procedure that requires continuous review of the functional nature of the activities involved, as well as the performance of the employee.

The "verification" tasks of the purchasing procedure mentioned earlier are continuous. Skills are delivered by the supplier/ employee and paid for on a regular basis. The events may seem automatic. They are, but you should be aware of the implications of these events. Each time a check is issued, it implies that skills were delivered by the employee in accordance with the purchaser's/employer's expectations. Verification of work hours, job performance, supervision and reviews, procedures for advancement and dismissal, are all parts of an organized purchasing function. They have their parallel in the purchase of nonhuman resources. Whether in a formal way or not, verification steps have to be performed in order to assure that the productivity of the resources is comparable to the expectations of the organization as expressed in its budgets and plans. While most of the verification tasks in personnel purchasing may not necessarily be a part of the financial management role, it is important to understand that they are essentially the same as with other resources.

To begin a contractual relationship with a new employee, a written statement or job description should be made about the position, the employer's expectations, the salary, and the starting and ending dates. Contracts can be renewed annually. They do not go on forever and ever. If the organization or project is subject to erratic funding or other funding problems, that situation should be made known as a condition of the employee's acceptance. In that way, uncertainty about the future can be clearly understood and contractual liability of the employer can be limited. The possible financial obligations to employees from misrepresentation, which ultimately fall on those who are legally responsible for the organization, may be avoided. Changes in the functions being performed or expected to be performed may well constitute a recontracting procedure for the services of your employee. Clarity about changes in job description or expectations helps avoid confusion about working relationships and contractual obligations. Furthermore, in growing organizations, it reinforces a procedure of review by managers, not only of the particular tasks of an employee but also of the shifting emphasis of different organizational functions.

PAYROLL-RELATED TRANSACTIONS

Because employment contracts are interrelated with other concerns such as fringe benefits, taxes, and regulatory controls, it is important to maintain a complete record of all transactions involving them. The employment laws require payments into certain insurance funds—social security and Worker's Compensation—and the income tax laws require timely payments to the Internal Revenue Service. These and other taxes, health insurance payments, pension fund, and the like may be applicable, depending on organization policy and state laws.

It is important to distinguish between fringe benefits, mandatory insurance, and employment taxes. These are often lumped together under the general title of "fringe" benefits, or compensation added to a basic salary. Employment taxes and mandatory insurance are legally required costs of employing an individual. A fringe benefit is an additional form of compensation particularly related to your workplace. It may be the result of an organizational requirement or policy, but it is not a legal or governmental requirement. A medical insurance program is usually a fringe benefit if paid in part or totally by the employer; so is a pension plan, and paid holidays in addition to legal ones. If an employee pays for these items, they are not a fringe benefit of the organization.

PAYING WITH CASH

Any group or organization, whatever its size, has to make small purchases during a week's activities that cannot be handled on a supplier billing basis as described earlier. Nor are such purchases easily made with checks. A "petty cash fund" is a device for having cash available to make purchases. But "Petty Cash" is not a budget category or line item. It is a method of payment. All purchases can be related to a specific budget allocation—such as office supplies, food, postage, or transportation—according to the resource needs of the project. Insofar as these and other categories of expenditures may require immediate payment, an available cash fund facilitates the process of making certain purchases. Cash funds should be set up to support specific activities or diverse functions, depending on purchasing conditions and program needs.

In terms of control of a cash fund, the same functions of authorization, delegation, verification, collection of receipts, and payment are necessary to make sure funds are not lost or misused. The administrator delegates a particular person to handle the fund. Requests are made to that person to use the funds. They are approved or disapproved in accordance with the purpose of the fund. If an item is purchased, a receipt should be presented (when available) to the fund manager. Reimbursement is made. A record of purchases is kept by the manager, regardless of the availability of receipts. The person who made the purchase initials the item in the record. The initials in effect say, "I made the purchase, and I have been reimbursed." The fund manager makes all the approvals and controls the cash. The fund manager is responsible to the administrator or some other delegating person such as the business manager or treasurer.

The actual mechanics of setting up a petty cash fund are fairly simple. A small amount of money, related to the use and turnover of the fund, should be determined. Limits on the size of individual purchases are set to separate small ones from larger ones that can or should be made by check. A check is made out to "cash," or to the fund manager with a notation that it is for a certain type of expenditure, such as office supplies, transportation, or food. The money is placed in a locked drawer or box. Only the fund manager should have access to the money. As funds are used up, a new check is issued, based on the record of expenditures as kept by the fund manager. In effect, the fund is reimbursed. The administrator reviews the list of expenditures before giving his or her OK to the issuance of a replenishment check.

The best management of such a fund in terms of staff is on a reimbursement basis, rather than providing funds before a purchase is made. In this way, the fund manager does not have to reimburse for inappropriate purchases, or be drawn into unnecessary arguments. While such purchases are in small amounts, the issues of accountability, control, and recording of expenditures have nothing to do with size. Loss, misuse, and theft are your concern as a financial manager or administrator. A recording procedure, set up for all cash transactions and for all individuals involved in the organization or project, will translate this concern into effective management (see Figure 7, "Cash Fund Record").

Is There a Question of "Trust?"

"Don't you trust me?" is often a common response to setting up a formal procedure for using "petty" cash. You may hear cries of "alienation," "bureaucracy," "big business," and so forth. They are for the most part irrelevant, or based on a lack of understanding about why a formal procedure is useful. As an organization grows, more maps are needed so decision-making responsibilities can be delegated and people can know what is expected of them. Regardless of size or type of organization, the authorization process helps assure that errors in spending are minimized, records are produced to validate expenditures, and there is a focal point from which lines of management control and corresponding accountability can be drawn.

Financial records should exist independent of changing personalities, methods of payment, and organizational forms. To provide documentation for what you or others have done with money that is not yours is or should be a mechanical process. Financial documentation helps provide a measure of individual and organizational accountability, as related to the implementation of project or program. In a larger scope, there is a serious moral and professional issue if you are unable to document and control expendi-

Date	Expenditure	Amount	Name
9/1/81	Beginning Balance	$25.00	
9/2	Small tools	$ 3.10	Henry S.
9/4	Office supplies	.79	Gail P.
9/4	Paint	1.79	Henry S.
9/7	Bus fare	1.25	Gail P.
9/8	Office supplies	2.18	Gail P.
9/9	Postage	2.40	Janet L.
9/11	Party treats	4.60	Janet L.
9/14	Bathroom supplies	2.85	Gail P.
9/15	Typewriter ribbon	3.30	Gail P.
9/16	Coffee (for parents)	4.80	Janet L.
9/18	New deposit	+25.00	
9/22	Xerox	3.96	Phillip C.
9/24	Children's games	6.40	Janet L.
9/28	Scissors	3.10	Henry S.
	Subtotal	$ 36.22	
	Balance	$ 13.78	

FIGURE 7. Cash fund record.

tures of money that is not your own, regardless of the amount. If a system is clear, well-defined, and used uniformly throughout the organization, fears about not being trusted will rapidly diminish.

CONTROL THROUGH SUPPLIERS

If you are to make purchases of a category of items (food, office supplies, services) on a regular basis, it is valuable to establish a relationship with an individual supplier. Sometimes you can negotiate a discount for promising all your business to one supplier. At least you can normally arrange for monthly billing rather than paying cash each time something is needed. In effect, the supplier is providing a short-term line of credit. Monthly billing will reduce

69

paperwork, enable you to pay with one check, and provide a record of purchases from the supplier. If you delegate purchasing authority to someone in the organization, that person's requests can be designated as the only ones that the vendor may honor. In this way, a vendor can help you maintain control over the purchasing process. However, the management tasks of authorization, verification, and approval are still the same; they have to be carried out to assure the validity of each transaction.

Such arrangements with vendors imply a responsibility on your part. Reasonably prompt payment of bills is expected by the vendor and you have the obligation to meet this expectation. There are times when funding is delayed or short-term financial problems arise. Most vendors will appreciate your honesty in telling them directly that there will be a delay in payment, rather than avoiding their notices and phone calls. Vendors of goods and services are not very different from your employees in their expectations about being paid or about the value of their products to you. You have obligations to pay if you accept their products.

PROCESSING THE OBLIGATIONS

The administrator's approval (or that of a delegated person) of the final bill for purchases of services or products marks the closing of the purchasing process. This final approval can be seen as an organizational review and control mechanism. As long as the services and products have been delivered and accepted, and the bill is consistent with the offer, a contract has been made. There is a legal obligation on the part of the organization to pay the bill.

A late or untimely protest of a bill without a solid reason is suspect and may create a poor credit reputation for your organization. That could mean that vendors will only sell on a cash basis. Consequently, a regular time for bill review, at the end of each week, should be set aside to systematize the process of bill approval. This review will allow the administrator or financial manager to be fully informed, on a timely basis, of the flow of individual purchases and obligations.

6

Payments and Receipts

The processing of approved bills for payment begins with an orderly collection of them in a "current" unpaid bills file kept by the bookkeeper or someone who will be preparing checks. In a small organization, the administrator usually approves the bills while writing checks. But as an organization grows larger, the approval is separated from the check issuance, because more people are involved in the authorization and payment processes. As the bookkeeping function develops it includes the tasks of systematic collection and recording of bills, receipts, and other purchase data, and making sure that they are approved for payment. Consequently, the approved bill must move from the control of the administrator or his or her delegate to the person in charge of processing approved bills and "issuing" checks for timely payment to vendors.

A "current-month" file of paid and unpaid bills does not necessarily contain all the month's expenses. Salaries, if there are no time sheets, rent, and petty cash or other cash-fund outlays, will only appear in the checkbook or register. There are often no

71

bills for these expenditures. Implicit or explicit approval will have to have been given for issuance of these checks.

Because most businesses send their bills at the end of the month and banks issue statements on a 30-day basis, you can integrate your records and payment activities with other systems on a monthly basis. More important, the maintenance of the financial records of an organization on a monthly basis provides timely information for you as an administrator and those to whom you are accountable. It may also meet other management requirements such as submission of reimbursement and funding documentation and financial reports to a governance committee or the board of directors as well as the managerial staff.

Short-term programs may require shorter payment and recordkeeping periods. A summer camp operation is the type of project where weekly financial reports may be needed for effective financial management. Banks require daily financial reports.

THE CHECKBOOK: PART OF THE AUTHORIZATION PROCESS

A checking account is an instrument of control of funds, as well as a payments device and a record of expenditures. All funds that come into an organization or project should be immediately deposited into the account to avoid misplacement or loss and to help provide an accurate record of available cash. There should never be any exception to this rule, even though cash may be needed for an emergency purpose. Only by passing all revenues and payments through a checking account can there possibly be a complete record of and full control over all funds handled by an organization. Those funds are payments for all products and services provided by the organization. Flexibility to make purchases can be maintained through the use of cash funds and reimbursement directly to individuals who document authorized purchases.

Aside from the fact that a properly signed check is an authorization for a bank to make a payment to someone, a signature on a check can signify the fulfillment of various organizational functions:

1. It is an *authorization* to pay by a representative delegated to act for the organization or a group.

2. It can indicate a final *review* and approval of purchases by the manager and other delegated persons.
3. It can provide *security* to another signer and to the organization.

It is common for administrators to act as signing agents of checks for their organizations. But since the administrator or project director is an employee of the organization with delegated authority to spend funds for the organization's activities, it is preferable that check signing be done by at least one other person. If you are the sole signer of checks that benefit you or for large purchases— your salary, reimbursements, and other expenditures—you risk your reputation. Questions of conflict of interest, or improper authorization of expenditures, can be raised. Thus officers of a corporation, trustees, or organizationally appointed representatives other than yourself are the proper signers of checks. Their signatures are to represent organizational approval, reflecting a review of purchases and the proper use of the authority to make them. But if there is no formal board of directors or trustees, there should be some persons other than the manager who is authorized to sign checks. Members of an operations committee, an advisory group, or a collective decision-making body are the appropriate signers, as long as they have ultimate responsibility for the financial management of the organization.

Whenever checks are prepared for signing, they should be accompanied by the bills or receipts for the services or goods they represent. These bills or receipts are information for the signer. They should have been reviewed by the administrator or delegated person prior to the final approval and signatures of the check signers as part of the payments authorization process. In this way the financial control function and organization review is cycled back to its origin!

From the perspective of the financial manager's role, it is desirable to use checks requiring two signatures, because the responsibility for payments is then shared. When others sign checks, no one in an organization or outside of it can accuse you of benefiting personally or making unauthorized expenditures. From the perspective of those who are responsible for the governance of the organization, their signatures are control over the expenditure of funds. An exception to this two-signature rule may be made for small purchases or for reimbursement of cash funds. This should be formal authorization, set up by those in the organization responsible for the financial management—the treasurer or an operations committee. In this way managerial flexibility is maintained and the possibility of questionable payments is limited.

THE CHECKBOOK AS A RECORD OF PAYMENTS AND RECEIPTS

You want to clearly show each checkbook transaction in order to maintain an understandable record of payments and deposits, regardless of their size. As your organizational activities develop from requiring just a banking account with a few dollars to a detailed operating budget, a more useful check-recording system will be needed than is offered in a simple checkbook with its stubs for noting payment details.

A "one-write" disbursements system, illustrated in Figure 8, is designed for more accurate and systematic recording of payments and deposits. It is a flexible data-collection system that incorporates bookkeeping procedures with the maintenance of essential financial records. The system utilizes regular bank checks with a carbon strip on the back. As a check is written, a record is imparted on a standard accounting form. Filling in stubs or separate records is unnecessary. The forms come in sizes of eight, twelve, and twenty columns. These columns are in addition to space provided for the usual check information—dates, name of payee, amount, and deposit information. The columns allow you to note the amount of the check in a single list arranged by date of issue, as well as in a budget matrix. By classifying each column as a budget category or line item, a breakdown ("budget spread") of payments and receipts is at your fingertips.

This record is a "disbursements" journal, a critical accounting reference. Each check is an "entry" in the journal. Each journal page shows a record of payments listed by date and number that can be classified according to budget allocations. Monthly bank statements of canceled checks and deposits are reconciled easily with this journal.

If your organization has many projects, payments in the journal can be shown as they are allocated to each project. One or several columns can be for a specific project. Each column might represent line items or categories of project expenditures. As payments are allocated to different projects and budgetary components within a project, the levels of expenditures by project are

Date	Payment to: (Disbursement)	Check Amount	Check No.	Account Balance Opening	Deposit	Salaries	Fringe	Phones	Supplies	Rent	Advertising	Printing	Travel	Insurance	
	Check No. 197														
	Check No. 198														
	Check No. 199														
	Check No. 200														
	Child Abuse & Treatment Street Address Town, State, Zip Code														
3/4/81	ABC Realty March Rent	$100.00	200							100.00					
	Town Bank & Trust Address	*Signature* *Signature*													
	TOTALS		Closing												

FIGURE 8. The "one-write" recording system check register.

readily available. The information from the check description column can be related to a more detailed budget.

Payroll records and vendor billing files can be integrated with this system. A special card, bearing the payee's name, can be inserted between the check and the journal to make another carbon-copy record of the information written on the check. The card becomes a full record of purchases and payments to individual persons or suppliers when purchase order numbers or billing statements are referenced to a specific payment. One-write systems offer numerous subsystems for making and receiving payments, as well as for other records of billing and receiving. The use of various forms and subsystems depends on the nature of the financial activities and the accounting records required by the organization and its funding sources. But the basic one-write disbursements system with a separate payroll record is adequate for most needs and is reasonably priced. Bookkeeping time and copying errors are substantially reduced. Financial information is better organized and simplified for different financial reporting and control purposes. Some national business systems suppliers are Safeguard Systems, Shaw Walker, and McBee Systems. You can probably find out from your local bank who supplies these or other systems in your area. They all provide a similar service.

CASH AND ACCRUAL ACCOUNTING

The type of information derived from the checkbook or register introduces a major financial reporting problem which in accounting terminology refers to types of information: cash and accrual basis of accounting. The problem arises from the recognition of the difference between paid, and the total of paid and unpaid obligations incurred during a given operating period. The check register or disbursements journal only shows payments. A financial report using only information from this source is misleading if there are significant amounts of unpaid obligations that are due or outstanding. The charges that have been incurred against budget items are understated if the amounts of unpaid obligations that can be allocated to those items are not recognized.

If you look at some of the budget items in Table 2, this problem can be illustrated as shown in Table 5. A report (I) from the records of the check register or disbursements journal would show that the project seems to be doing well. After three months, costs

TABLE 5. Budget Items

	Budget for First 3 months	Payments shown in check register	I Variance Budget/Actual	Payments & unpaid bills	II Variance Budget Items
Rent $200/mo.	$ 600	$ 600	$ 0	$ 600	$ 0
Telephone $50/mo.	150	125	+ 25	170	– 20
Office Supplies $25/mo.	75	60	+ 15	95	– 20
Advertising Personnel $500	500	420	+ 80	525	– 25
Travel $30/mo.	90	65	+ 25	110	– 20
	$1,415	$1,270	+$145	$1,500	–$85

are less than had been anticipated. You would appear to be a good administrator.

But the opposite picture is revealed when the unpaid obligations are taken into account. In the second calculation (II), charges to each budget item are greater than the amounts projected for the period in review. The differences are significant, especially if you consider that you are already overspending in the first three months of the project. Furthermore, suppose you knew that there were other bills for the same period which had arrived after the report was completed, or were on your desk for approval —let's say $30 for advertising and $15 for office supplies. Also, one of the staff had lost his travel voucher of $15 for the third month. He is making out a new one for your review and approval. All these charges, technically, should be allocated to the first three months because goods and services were consumed or acquired during that time. Actually, you have overspent your budget by $85 + $60, or $145. This is equal to more than 10 percent of the projected or budgeted expenditures. Information from the check register would still indicate that the activities are costing less than expected, when the opposite is in fact true.

A financial report reflects the accounting method that is used. The *accrual basis* of accounting requires the recording of liabilities as an "expense" as soon as the *benefits* (goods and services) are received. Income is recorded when earned rather than when received. Both bills owed (obligations) and income are recognized when they occur, regardless of when they are paid or received. The *cash basis* of accounting (I) only recognizes obligations when they are paid, and income when it is received.

In the purchasing process described in prior pages, you noted that a supplier's billing for goods and services must coincide with what is actually received by the organization. In effect, the benefit to the purchaser and the bill from the supplier have to be consistent. Since there is often a time lag between delivery and billing, a supplier may be providing monthly credit. Sometimes that billing process is delayed because of organizational or personal procedures, or lack thereof. Verifications, approvals, payments, and billings are not instantaneous on either side of a transaction. But the accrual basis of accounting, as it is being interpreted here, indicates that as soon as a bill comes for products and services delivered, it is counted as an expenditure (a charge-to-a-budget item) as long as it is not disputed. Within this commercial framework, your organization, through its verification procedures, may delay the final recognition until there is an administrative approval prior to making out the payment check. But delay beyond a reasonable time, often stated on a bill, is not assumed by the vendor. Once the bill is accepted, there is a contractual liability. Thus, the administrative function of approving bills should be done on a timely basis, to provide current financial information and continuity between purchasing, confirming obligations, and making payments.

WHY THE DIFFERENCES IN ACCOUNTING METHODOLOGY?

If you had sufficient funds to pay all your bills at the end of each month all the time, the disbursements journal would indeed record all expenses for your activities. Bills that accrued during the month or some other specified time period would be paid at the end of the month, or sooner, as required. There would be no unpaid obligations outstanding. Current financial status of a program would be reported with assuredness. Charges to a budget item would be fully paid. The criteria of accuracy in financial reporting would be met. So the answer to the question of methodology is the following:

> Under the circumstances where incoming funds of an organization (project) are usually sufficient to meet monthly expenses as they occur, a cash basis of accounting will meet accounting and financial reporting needs of management.

Because much funding of small nonprofit organizations is on a reimbursement basis, an accrual system is usually necessary because many bills are held until funds arrive from funding sources. For whatever reason, as long as revenues come into an organization differently from the flow of obligations, and lags in payments result, the differences between the two must be accounted for and clearly understood by all those responsible for managing and directing an organization's activities.

The accrual basis of accounting arises out of the needs for accurate reporting of financial status of activity when the cash basis cannot show all the charges or obligations to the budget. The accrual basis accounts for the expenditures as they are incurred, eliminating the dangerous problem of not recognizing financial obligations until after they have been paid.

Application of accrual-based accounting among small nonprofit organizations is most realistic on a modified basis. While obligations are charged when they are incurred, potential revenues are not accounted for until actually received. Thus possible misleading overstatements of "available" resources, resulting from optimistic expectations about the flow of revenues into an organization, are avoided. The author's own experience leads him to believe that the only funds you can count on being available for operations are those you have in your bank account. Technically, even deposits of checks have to be "cleared"—paid out by the check-issuing bank—before they constitute available resources. Checks sometimes bounce. As a practical matter, expectations of receipts—i.e., promised donations, reimbursements, and even contractual obligations to pay—are not a substitute for actual moneys in the bank. Thus a conservative view about the amount and timing of incoming revenues, combined with a realistic treatment of obligations, will spare those responsible for money matters considerable grief when they are planning expenditures and paying bills.

Because expenses are tracked from their time of contractual obligation, accrual accounting will go a long way to help prevent "surprises" about running big deficits in budgets and specific budget items, as shown on page 82 in the illustration. Of course, if unpaid bills pile up on a manager's desk, awaiting his or her approval, or "disappear" between the times of receipt and approval, they can never arrive at the bookkeeper's desk for recording and payments processing. No accounting method will produce accurate results if administrative procedures are absent or are not followed. Financial reports clearly reflect continuity of information flows through the purchasing system, as well as the payments system.

In the final analysis, whoever is responsible for the organization must see that the administrator or managers carry out all their approval functions on a timely basis and that all notices of financial obligation are efficiently recorded and processed. The whole financial reporting mechanism and purpose begins and ends with a chain of their authorization to make purchases and approval with the signing of a check.

REIMBURSEMENT REPORTING

As already indicated, a monthly collection of approved bills and the disbursements journal or check register will provide the source of information for submission of reimbursement vouchers. The *voucher* is a bill to the reimbursing agency for *expenditures* (costs) which your organization has incurred in implementing a contracted program. Vouchers are usually submitted on a monthly basis. You want your voucher to include all the obligations you have incurred, during the specific time period, even though actual payments of the bills may be less. The total costs incurred during the period represent costs of resources you have acquired in order to deliver goods and services in support of activities. Some refunding sources restrict reimbursement only to paid bills, thereby disregarding the nature of the expenditure. If a reimbursement arrangement is based on this condition, the cash requirements of the organization will be increased substantially. From an accountability view, the funding source should be satisfied with evidence of your obligations, not payments.

As shown earlier, the obligations are legally binding on your organization. However, just because your organization incurs an obligation, that does not mean that it will be automatically reimbursed! The reimbursement arrangement is usually one in which the funding source controls the program expenditures through its own review and approval procedures. The funding source has final say as to whether expenditures are being appropriately made according to prior agreement.

Often the management control procedures and perspective of the funding source are no different from the one discussed on the management of a cash fund. As a manager of an organization, you stand in the same relation to the administrator of a funding source as the petty cash manager stands in relation to you. The management control activities of authorization, review, and repayment is also needed by the funding source where a reimbursement is involved. The funding-source administration is accountable to those who delegated spending authority to it—i.e., a legislature, trustees, a dispensing agent. The funding organization is accountable to the legislature in the same way that you, the financial manager, are accountable to your board of directors.

The reimbursement voucher can be a financial report as well as a bill to the funding source insofar as it provides a detailed list of expenditures. The same information is part or even all of the financial report of your organization each month. It is "part of" when the organization's budget is larger than the project component being reimbursed. Otherwise, it is the same information. A voucher should be in the same budget language as used in the original contract. If it is not, the data will be confusing to the staff of the funding agency. You are not obligated in any way to show other financial information of the organization's budget unless you have a contractual requirement to do so.

When you submit your reimbursement requests, you may

also want to include a separate funding statement of how many of your past vouchers have been reimbursed, and what is outstanding, excluding the current submission. Such information may be important to relay in writing to your funding representative, especially if he or she is part of a large organization. The status of reimbursements may not be known and the information provides a written communication to the funding source.

If your organization is heavily dependent on this type of financing, it is important for you, as an administrator, and the board members to know the status of reimbursements. Delays in

FIGURE 9. The Manager's overview.

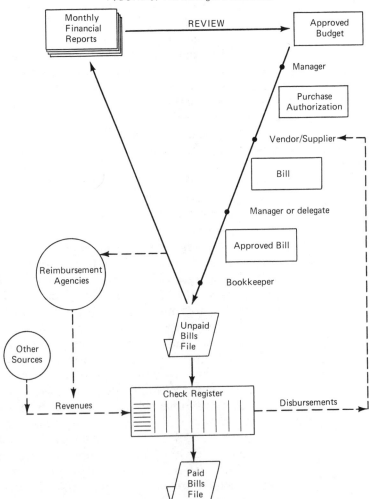

reimbursements may cause considerable difficulties in paying high-priority obligations such as salaries, telephone bills, and so forth. Consequently, attention should be given to follow-up of the processing of vouchers. Keep a record of submission dates, amounts, and voucher numbers. Timely submission of the voucher with accurate information is your responsibility. The benefit of giving your attention to a well-prepared voucher may be a reduction in processing delays and confusion on the part of the payor.

As reimbursement funds flow into the organization, payments of past outstanding obligations can be made. Paid and unpaid bills should be kept separately to avoid mix-ups and double payments, but more important, to provide immediate knowledge of outstanding obligations at any time. A comparison of the amount of unpaid bills with the balance in the organization's checking account shows your capability of meeting current, pressing obligations or imminent expenditures such as salaries.

Your organization is a financial intermediary between funding sources and the sellers of resources. Figure 9, "The Manager's Overview," shows the basic internal functions previously discussed as they are related to financial flows to and from the organization including reimbursement financing.

REVENUES AND RECEIPTS

As noted earlier, all funds received by an organization should be passed through the checking account. If incoming funds are not recorded, not only will revenues appear to be less than they actually are, but, viewed as the financial valuation of the resources used up in the programs, they will also be understated. Unrecorded funds used to pay bills to acquire resources that were not budgeted distorts the picture of activities' costs and financial reporting. Thus the central idea is that all funds generated by the use of assets of the organization should be returned to the organization in such a way that there is a complete record and control of them. If there are a limited number of revenue transactions such as monthly reimbursements, a separate record of receipts need not be maintained as long as they can be adequately shown in the checkbook records. But if there are numerous individual payments for different products or services, then a journal of individual receipts is desirable and necessary. By recording receipts systematically in terms of the services or products that have been sold, you can accurately relate income and expenditures of specific programs or activities to one another. The financial management objective is to be able to analyze individual projects or activities to determine if revenues are enough to meet budgeted expenses, or are producing surpluses. Some detailed revenue records may have to be maintained for tax purposes, such as transactions involving sales. Nonprofit tax exemption status does not automatically preclude the requirement for collection and payment of sales taxes.

As mentioned earlier, a "modified" accrual basis of accounting for and reporting of revenues helps provide a realistic attitude toward planning expenditures and paying bills. It also provides a sound basis for viewing revenues. Since a major funding method for small nonprofit organizations is donations and gifts, it is important that you understand that promises from donors are usually not legally binding. Experienced managers know that many an expected donation has never materialized. The best policy is to make no assumptions about such promises of revenues. Cash and the "modified" accrual reporting basically say that only when funds are received by an organization can they be treated as revenues. As a working practice, promises of donations should be politely and carefully followed up. But if they are not bankable within a week or two, forget them.

Another management concern that is often present in small nonprofit organizations is the handling of incoming cash. Easy access to cash provides too much of a temptation for some people. Preventing theft, loss, or misuse in handling cash can usually be accomplished by involving more than one person in the receiving and recording tasks. Consider the mechanism used by movie theaters. One person sells a ticket and receives cash, another person counts (accounts for) sales indirectly by keeping part of the ticket stub. In a similar way, issuing receipts for cash for your organization's activities is to maintain a verifying record. Also, by having two people count money, there is less likelihood of its disappearance.

7

The Different Uses of
Financial Information

FINANCIAL REPORTS:
TWO PERSPECTIVES

If you are a manager, board member, representative, or in any role that involves overseeing the financial management of an organization, it is incumbent upon you to have and regularly use financial reports. It is, in fact, a matter of utmost importance that an organization have financial information available that is timely, accurate, and most of all understandable to everyone associated with its efforts and activities, particularly those responsible for the governance functions.

On the other hand, the institutions that fund small nonprofit organizations usually require that the potential recipients submit some type of financial statements that verify past use of funds. These statements are often annual reports that are "certified" by an independent, professionally licensed public accountant. Such reports constitute financial validation of the way the organization has spent its funds in the past, rather than having anything to do with financial management per se. These data are sometimes used to make decisions about new and continued funding of activities.

85

In the managerial situation above, the information reference is to operations reports; and in the funding-source situation, the reference is to financial reports of how funds have been used. The latter constitute a formal "accounting" for resources acquired for producing activities during a period of time, usually a year. They are prepared by someone with extensive professional training who seems at times to employ a foreign language to explain, summarize, and organize financial transactions. For simplicity and only for purposes of this book, further references to financial "statements" will mean only those reports that are prepared by a professional accountant. Thus, a general distinction can be made between accountants' formal reporting documents and other financial reports.

WHAT MUST BE ACCOUNTED FOR

There are four questions concerning financial information about the use of resources that we consider in decision making; and it is according to one of these that the accountant focuses his or her efforts to organize and measure financial transactions of an organization.

1. What are the resources controlled by the organization and how are they financed? (Balance Sheet)
2. How were these resources used for products and service, and how much revenues did they generate? (Profit and Loss Statement for a specific time period.)
3. What are the periodic changes in the amounts of resources available and changes in financial obligations and funding?
4. What is the amount of surplus or loss from use of resources periodically, and how does it affect the sources of financing? (Statement of Surplus or Retained Earnings)

These questions are not significantly different from what you can ask yourself about your own personal financial situation. Just think in terms of use of your annual income and the surplus or "loss" financed with savings, loans, or gifts.

1. What do you own and owe at any given date? Do you have a savings account, a car, a house, some stocks or bonds, a paid-for retirement plan or other "assets"? What did you pay for them or what are they worth? Any possessions that you own

are your resources, even though you may be still paying creditors for them. How much do you owe on the same date? The difference between the value of what you own and what you owe is your "net worth," your "personal worth."

2. How do you use your income to support your "lifestyle" or that of your family? Food, rent, and clothes are the most common expenditures, but there is also education, entertainment, books, sports, insurance, helping others in the family, or making donations to a religious affiliation or local organization. This does not concern how you budget your spending, but how you in fact spent your money (used up your resources) during a specific period of time.

3. What about the changes in income and expense patterns from pay raises, retirement, unemployment, inheritance, and other factors, or from sudden major expenses for medicine or house repairs, and the availability of loans for new purchases? How these effect our savings and other resources, and the changes in the debts that financed them is measured periodically too. Thus at the end of any given period of time, there is a new total of assets from surplus income, new acquisitions, or disposal of resources and a new total of debts.

4. How much is the annual surplus or loss and how does that affect the net worth? While corporations earn profits that may be distributed to owners or reinvested in the business, individuals may have surplus funds above their expenses during any given time period. Though what they "need to live on" may be much more flexible than they think, there are necessary expenses. They often have some relatively "fixed" costs for resources—i.e., mortgage payments for shelter, and daily expenses that are essential but vary widely depending on tastes and conditioning (e.g., food and clothes). Some people let their "extra" money accumulate in their checking account or in a cookie jar. Others try to manage their surplus moneys by investing in various types of assets— savings accounts, stocks and bonds, real estate, and so forth. Education may also be included as an "investment" when it is preparation for earning future income. Sometimes we pay ourselves our own "dividend," a distribution of surplus funds, by taking a special vacation. We may invest our surplus in new resources or consume it, if there is any. Sometimes we have to use up our savings or borrow to meet expenses. Then we reduce our assets and our "net worth."

Your organization may derive income from many sources, and use it to produce a variety of goods and services. Its financial statements show that during a year, the costs of resources to produce the output was so much. There may be unused resources at the end of that year as well as unpaid debt and funds owed to it. In these reports, output is measured periodically, by revenues or income received for it. The costs of resources used to produce the revenues is subtracted to determine a surplus or deficit. Changes in the available resources, and debt to finance them, is also measured periodically and reported cumulatively for the correspondent date of the end of the income reporting period. "Profits" are surplus revenues over costs of resources used up for a given amount of production which is sold to other users or consumers. They are one of several sources to finance the acquisition of additional resources. Profits do not have to exist to have socially and economically valuable output. Our concern is the acquisition and use of resources and the flow of revenues to pay for them. Financial management tools provide controls and information about surpluses and deficits.

These same four questions apply to all profit or nonprofit organizations, and for the most part, the accountant goes about responding to them in the same way. The work is best performed when the needs of the various users are met without compromises and without slanting of the information for any particular party's use or argument (see Figure 10, "Financial Information Users"). The accounting profession has developed uniform standards for measuring the transaction in order to organize and present this information as fairly as possible.

Figure 11 illustrates the flow of resources through an organization as represented by the four accounting measures of financial transactions.

FIGURE 10. Financial information users.

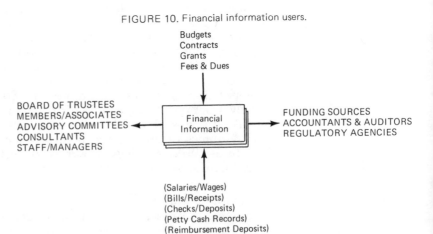

BOARD OF TRUSTEES
MEMBERS/ASSOCIATES
ADVISORY COMMITTEES
CONSULTANTS
STAFF/MANAGERS

Budgets
Contracts
Grants
Fees & Dues

Financial
Information

FUNDING SOURCES
ACCOUNTANTS & AUDITORS
REGULATORY AGENCIES

(Salaries/Wages)
(Bills/Receipts)
(Checks/Deposits)
(Petty Cash Records)
(Reimbursement Deposits)

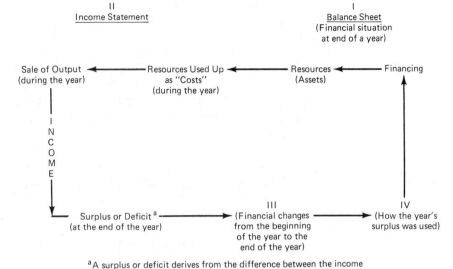

FIGURE 11. Financial-flow diagram.

II
Income Statement

I
Balance Sheet
(Financial situation
at end of a year)

Sale of Output ← Resources Used Up ← Resources ← Financing
(during the year)   as "Costs"   (Assets)
                    (during the year)

I
N
C
O
M
E

Surplus or Deficit [a] → III (Financial changes → IV (How the year's
(at the end of the year) from the beginning   surplus was used)
                          of the year to the
                          end of the year)

[a] A surplus or deficit derives from the difference between the income
and the cost of resources to produce it. A surplus becomes available
to the owners to finance new resources. A deficit is a corporate
obligation for which the owners are responsible.

"BOOK"KEEPING

The key to developing financial reports is the maintenance of records about all transactions in an orderly and current manner that allows for their use for different organizational purposes. Bookkeeping is the crucial elementary function of financial management and financial reporting. However, bearing in mind the previously mentioned focus of the accountants' reports and the decision makers' needs, these "books" of transactions are designed to record and collate financial information in special ways. The information is usually reconstructed for managerial use.

A check "book" can be an informal bookkeeping system if it shows all the transactions of an organization with enough detail about the resources purchased and the revenue generated. The one-write bookkeeping method discussed in Chapter 6 systematizes the normal procedure of writing checks so there can be a formal record of the information that appears on the checkbook "stubs." These data can be distributed to budget items or categories of expenditures in the many columns of this "journal" or register. A daily record of transactions can easily be maintained. In essence, the individual columns are "books" of the same (rent) or similar (office supplies) transactions. Individual columns may also comprise categories of expenditures of particular programs or contracts. While the checkbook also shows deposits, to be an adequate accounting record, each transaction and source of the income would have to be identified. All payments to the organization (receipts) comprise the deposits. Receipts can be related to disbursements categories in the check register. A separate receipts "book" or journal is needed if there are many more than a dozen transactions a month.

Another very important part of your records, one that is required by the Internal Revenue Service and state agencies, is payroll information. This record provides your employees with tax and other information as well as meeting legal and reporting requirements of your organization. One-write disbursement systems can usually include a detailed record for these purposes, or a separate journal can be maintained. Your local bank can help provide all the information about salary withholding for unemployment insurance, Social Security, payroll taxes, and so forth. The banks handle payments to the state and federal government on a periodic basis.

Because the accounting focus is on measuring what resources were acquired and which were used, the bookkeeping tasks include records of not only the cash transaction but also their explanations. In accounting terminology this is known as "supporting documentation"—bills, petty cash receipts, contracts, and individual recordings of income or detailed deposit slips. Maintaining these records helps answer the question of what resources were acquired, where they came from, and if they were paid for. Periodic changes of resource availability and use are measurable as long as recording of this information is dated sequentially. A financial report can be compiled at any time by adding up or "summarizing" and categorizing transactions. Financial reports are in fact summaries of many transactions.

As an organization grows, its bookkeeping records may have to become more detailed because of the increased number of transactions. Electronic data processing (EDP) is a means of substituting hand calculations and entries to different records and reports. A computer printout of biweekly payroll transactions constitutes a payroll disbursements journal. Twenty-six computer printouts could make up the bookkeeper's record of payroll for a year (see Figure 12, "The Basic 'Books'").

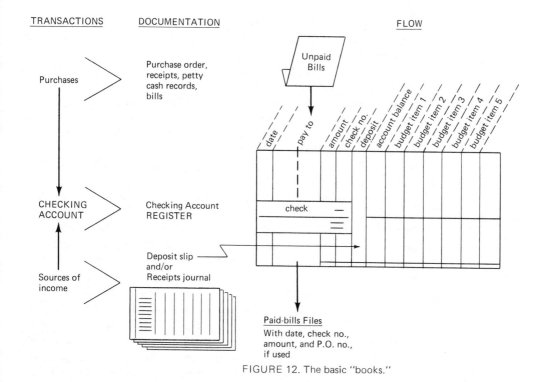

FIGURE 12. The basic "books."

ACCOUNTING: WHAT'S INVOLVED?

"To account for" resource expenditures is a professional service of a few and a practical concern of many if not all of us. Individually, many people keep some financial records, particularly for tax purposes. They have a citizen's responsibility to do so. For ease and reliability, much of this task is relegated to employers for the purposes of maintaining payroll records and making deductions. Once the government gets its share of your personal income, decisions about how to spend the remaining money are your own business. But on an organizational basis, when you are spending other people's money, whether it be from government contracts, tax-deductible donations, membership fees and dues, or stockholders' capital, you are accountable to others for your decisions. But the larger issue here is informed decision making about the use of resources in the society. Those charged with the spending and invest-

91

ment responsibility in both the public and private spheres have to rely on some type of reasonably accurate financial information about an activity in order to allocate resources.

Since an organization and its activities are ongoing, there is always unfinished use of resources. Because most data are subject to interpretation in both their compilation and review, accounting standards have been developed by the accounting profession to resolve questions about objectivity and relevance in evaluating resource utilization. Known as the GAAP, generally accepted accounting principles, these standards comprise a uniform system for both measurement and reporting.

A Certified Public Accountant (CPA) is an accountant licensed by the profession to provide independent verification of financial reports and supporting documentation. Such a verification is based on an "audit," an in-depth testing of transactions and controls. Audited financial reports are known as certified financial statements. In these reports, the CPA states a professional opinion about whether information is in conformity with GAAP and will specifically note problems of inconsistency and valuation. The ultimate concern is whether the statements, which summarize the multitude of transactions of an organization, present fairly the financial positions and results of its operations.

The audit is a procedure that establishes in-depth verification of information provided in a financial statement. The CPA's authority to speak independently is matched by the potential of professional liability for failure to exercise care and diligence in discovering departures from GAAP that may cause a user to suffer losses from reliance on the information. An unaudited financial statement, "compilations" of data, and professional "review" may conform to these principles, but they do not have the legal implications of an audited report. Any accountant licensed by the profession can provide professional credibility to financial information.

An experienced accountant can provide the technical assistance for establishing suitable recording systems which reflect the needs of particular activities, and assessing the treasury functions including but not limited to

1. Preparing and designing meaningful reports
2. Advice on internal controls in purchasing procedures, the collection and handling of income, and the organization of bookkeeping procedures and data compilation
3. Filing of taxes and other regulatory agency reports

4. Overall evaluation of performance of the financial management functions.

While not all accountants are CPAs, most of them are well qualified to organize and manage financial information and controls in the larger organizations and to set up bookkeeping and reporting systems for the need of managers and bookkeepers in small organizations. Uniform standards for bookkeeping exist, but individual recording systems are designed to reflect the types and flows of transactions of different activities and reporting requirements. Their forms are not a given for all organizations, though the data-collection orientation is the same. Reports derived from them must respond to the four questions expressed in the beginning of this chapter that are the focus of the accounting profession.

FINANCIAL INFORMATION USERS

The primary concern of people responsible for the management of an organization is and should be to have feedback about how their plans relate to the "real" world. They approved a plan of action and a budget, they authorized others to carry it out and act for the organization, and they should want to know what has happened. They are in fact legally "accountable" for the use of the funds. For that reason, all channels of information must flow to and from the authorizing representatives and the governance structure.

Timeliness, readibility, and accuracy are the criteria for information management. In an active organization, feedback is of little or no use if the latest data show what happened three months ago. The wider the gap between the report and the event, the greater the potential for loss of control, and the less meaningful is a managerial review. Thus *timeliness* of cycling information through and from the program and administrative activities is a requisite of organization health.

Most people who are involved with nonprofit organizations are uneasy when they hear the term "financial report." The visual experience must not further isolate them. If reports are not *designed to be understood* by the various users, most of whom are "nonfinancial people," they are useless for planning and control.

Though *accuracy* or *validity* have been mentioned before, it is worth repeating that these also represent a crucial element of data collection and reporting. Without being too philosophical, we can say that a considerable dimension of "validity" at the reviewer's level has to do with clarity and mutuality of meaning about information. Many people use professional words that they really do not understand or have a different meaning in the minds of others. While everyone *seems* to share an understanding of commonly used financial language, they in fact do not! This is particularly true in the financial field in the nonprofit sector, where there are relatively few financially oriented professionals, and their particular talents often seem to be undervalued.

The fact that a report excludes certain information does not necessarily mean it is inaccurate. The information may well be "accurate"—i.e., show the correct amount of bills paid—but it may be misleading if you really wanted to know or thought you were getting a report of total expenses including unpaid obligations outstanding. If you did not know the significance, it is not necessarily a fault of the information. For this author, many problems of making use of financial information and setting up internal controls have to do with the lack of knowledge about transaction flows and organization of data collection, rather than the narrow context of whether a particular figure is right or not. The usual concern of nonfinancial people is "What does the figure mean?" Only when they know what the numbers are supposed to interpret, since financial reports are abstractions, can they then make useful reviews and decisions.

Unfortunately, much financial reporting in nonprofit organizations is designed by accountants for accountants, rather than for managers, governance participants who are not accountants, and others responsible for both activities and organizational finances. You don't have to be a trained financial analyst or accountant to read and make use of most financial reports. There is no mystique in numbers, especially when you fully understand that they are measurements of costs of activities and functions, and the value that funding sources place on the products of your organization's programs. While the language of bookkeeping and accounting is new to many of us, it is mostly a set of professional labels for some common-sense organizational tasks and measurements. As you have already seen, a "journal" is a daily record of transactions. A "disbursements" journal is a daily record of payments. A payroll journal is a record of a specific *category* of payments.

Figure 13, "Transaction Flows," looks at the organization or program in terms of its continual life. The reports of financial

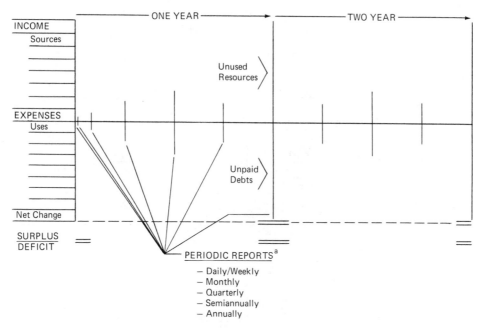

a The reporting period depends on the information and financial control requirements.

FIGURE 13. Transaction flows.

activity reflect the acquisition of resources for its products. A measure can be made of the resources used and income received for output of the product for any given time period. The reporting needs vary with the activities of the organization. The life of an organization will sooner or later terminate when the expense of the production is greater than the income from purchases of output including funding sources, creditors, and stockholders or boardmembers who refuse to finance a deficit.

MANAGEMENT INFORMATION

Essential financial information that a reporting function must produce for effective management is

1. A clear basis for periodic review of whether expenses and revenues of activities, projects, or overall programs are matching budgeted (expected) levels
2. A current picture of the available financial resources and an indication if the flow of revenues into and out of the organization is occurring as anticipated

BUDGET vs. ACTUAL EXPENDITURES

Budget Month 3

| Item | ANNUAL BUDGET[a] | YEAR–TO–DATE | | MONTH 3 |
		BUDGETED[b]	ACTUAL[c]	
PERSONNEL				
Program Coordinator	$13,700	$ 3,206	$ 2,915	$ 1,166
Secretary/Bookkeeper	7,170	1,168	1,168	667
Hotline Coordinator	8,955	1,458	1,458	833
Group Leader Assistant	4,750	250	250	250
PAC Coordinator	9,629	1,376	1,146	917
Assistant	7,269	519	519	519
FRINGE 20%	10,295	1,595	1,491	870
Subtotal	$61,768	$ 9,572	$ 8,947	$ 5,222
NONPERSONNEL				
Telephone				
hotline	$ 482	32	40	40
office	975	75	85	40
Supplies & Postage	310	85	80	45
Rent	1,100	200	200	100
Advertising	500	460	430	30
Printing	500	-0-	-0-	-0-
Travel	598	28	26	22
Insurance	600	600	-0-	-0-
UNALLOCATED	2,900			
	$69,433	$ 11,052	$ 9,808	$ 5,472

[a] The annual budget is composed of the 90-day start-up budget plus the expected monthly costs of full operation for the remaining nine months as calculated in Table 2.

[b] From Figure 5, The Start-up Budget

[c] The actual expenditures show that the program coordinator and the PAC coordinator were hired later than planned. Other expenditures were over and under their expected levels.

FIGURE 14A. Monthly Status Report.

The first perspective deals with a continuous verification of your financial maps with your experiences in the real world of resource acquisition and productivity. It relates anticipated costs and revenues to the actual expenditures and income. The comparison provides the structure of a financial status report that says "This is where we had planned to go" and "This is where we are." It may

BUDGET vs ACTUAL EXPENDITURES

Budget Month 3

Item	ANNUAL BUDGET	YEAR—TO—DATE		VARIANCE
		BUDGETED	ACTUAL	
PERSONNEL				
Program Coordinator	$13,700	$3,206	$2,915	+$291
Secretary/Bookkeeper	7,170	1,168	1,168	-0-
Hotline Coordinator	8,955	1,458	1,458	-0-
Group Leader Assistant	4,750	250	250	-0-
PAC Coordinator	9,629	1,376	1,146	+230
Assistant	7,269	519	519	-0-
FRINGE 20%	10,295	1,595	1,491	+104
Subtotal	$61,768	$9,572	$8,947	+$625
NONPERSONNEL				
Telephone				
hotline	482	32	40	-8
office	975	75	85	-10
Supplies & Postage	310	85	80	+5
Rent	1,100	200	200	-0-
Advertising	500	460	430	+30
Printing	500	-0-	-0-	-0-
Travel	298	28	26	+2
Insurance	600	600	-0-	+600
UNALLOCATED	2,900			
Total	$69,433	$11,052	$9,808	$1,244

FIGURE 14B. Variance Status Report.

raise questions about why you did not arrive at your financial location, which is really asking why you did not meet your program and operational objectives. What problems or lack of program information is being discovered as the activities are implemented that make resource requirements and financial estimates inaccurate?

Figures 14A & B, "Status Report," set forth a simple form for meeting basic financial reporting needs of both the management and in some instances outside parties. The first column of Figure 14A is the full budget of the organization; but it could be limited to the budget of specific program components or contracts, that require specified financial reporting to funding sources, or reimbursement requests. The first two columns are the projected budgeted costs. They are theoretical. Both the second and third

97

columns are cumulative to the end of the current reporting period which is noted on the "year-to-date" heading. The third column is composed of the cumulative actual expenditures, which also include the current month. The fourth column shows the income and expenses of the reporting period. Illustrated as a monthly report, this report could, however, show the "variances" between columns 2 and 3 as of the end of the reporting period. In Figure 14B, a variance report looks at the difference between cumulative projected and actual expenditures and revenues to date. This presentation emphasizes the cumulative difference between budgeted and actual expenses rather than the most recent transactions. Significant differences between items in these columns are a signal to managers and board members to ask questions about itemized or program expenditures, to re-evaluate costs of the functions or activities, and possibly to strengthen lines of delegation and accountability where necessary. Where revenue expectations are involved, a careful review of assumptions about them and the activities that were supposed to have produced them is necessary when the expected flow does not happen. This is especially critical when these funds are necessary to financing continued operations.

Are Projections Being Met?

"Re-evaluation" can be a significant activity here. The budget is based on a proposed structure of functions and activities, designed from a particular strategy, with an expectation about resource costs and utilization and revenue flows. Simply stated, the numbers in the budget reflect a particular plan of action. When significant variation occurs between what was budgeted and actual costs, resources are most likely not being acquired and utilized as expected, and objectives are not being achieved. The following are a few common explanations:

PLANNING FACTORS
- Actual costs of resources are much greater (less) than expected.
- Budgeted costs did not include important items.
- Essential functions, often managerial, were not calculated in the expected total cost of the project.
- Implementation may have taken much longer than expected; consequently, funds were spent at a lower rate, or vice versa.

- The program or parts of it simply cannot be implemented as planned; its strategy or design are not operative.

DATA-COLLECTION FACTORS

- Some bills for the period reported may not have arrived until after the latest report was presented, so actual costs are understated.
- Financial reporting is on a cash basis which may also understate actual costs.
- Costs and revenues of different projects are mixed together without clear explanation.
- Anticipated receipts are being treated as actual revenues.

These and other reasons often suggest questions about new policy, activities and strategy revisions, reporting methods, and other managerial procedures that have to be considered to achieve organizational strength and program objectives.

A start-up budget, as shown in Chapter 4, is composed of a series of added costs of resources as they are scheduled to produce new functions and activities. Each sequential reporting period will reflect added activity, as shown in Figure 5 (page 50).

Comparison of actual costs with the start-up financial plan of new activities provides a powerful review orientation at a critical stage of program and organizational development. Reread the section "The Magic of a 90-Day Budget," in Chapter Four, in the context of internal review and reporting functions. Think of yourself in different roles of organizational responsibility: executive director of a multiprogram operation, a board member or an active participant on an advisory committee, or even a representative of a funding source responsible for the success of this project.

Figure 14A may be used for reporting to a funding source or as a status report of a project. The fourth column would show the itemized list of monthly expenditures according to budget items in a contract. As reimbursement requests (vouchers), these reports usually require accompanying copies of the bills or canceled checks. Though cumulative data are usually not required by funding sources on a monthly basis, the vouchers presented as both a bill for expenses and a status report may be convenient and useful to the administrative officer. Since the calculation of all the columns is done for organizational reporting, any portion of the status report can easily be made available to a funding source as a more complete financial report that accompanies the reimbursement voucher.

Can the Bills be Paid?

A statement about the current cash position shows the net change in the amount of cash available for paying past and current bills that are outstanding since the last report, as well as the immediately expected disbursements such as payroll. It shows how much came into and how much was paid out of the checking account on a cumulative and periodic basis. It may be for one project or a composite of several projects and programs. A detailed breakdown of these changes and source of funds by project is essentially what a "funds balance" report is all about. If receipts and expenditures in the checking account or register are arranged according to individual activities or contracted services and their related funding sources, then the receipts and payments flows of each component of the organization's budget can be clearly seen. The checking-account balance at the end of any time period is the sum of the net changes in receipts and payments occurring for each project, plus the ending balance from the previous report. If the expected flows of revenues and expenditures are not on budget targets, then the manager must take immediate action with board members to secure funds or stop activities or both. Detailed reporting focuses on specific areas and indirectly on assumptions that they have contributed to the situation. It is the board's ultimate responsibility to take charge when bills are not being paid.

FUND BALANCES

A fund balance report is particularly important where funding is restricted and on a reimbursement basis. Lags in reimbursement receipts will become evident to reviewers. The overall accounting concern is that when payments and revenues are recorded in the checking-account register in accordance with individual projects or funding sources, restricted funds can be segregated from one another and accounted for; they can be maintained in one checking account. The job of accounting for financial flows into and out of different projects or activities is also accomplished without much searching and questioning. The fears funding sources have about "commingling"—mixing funds indiscriminately without

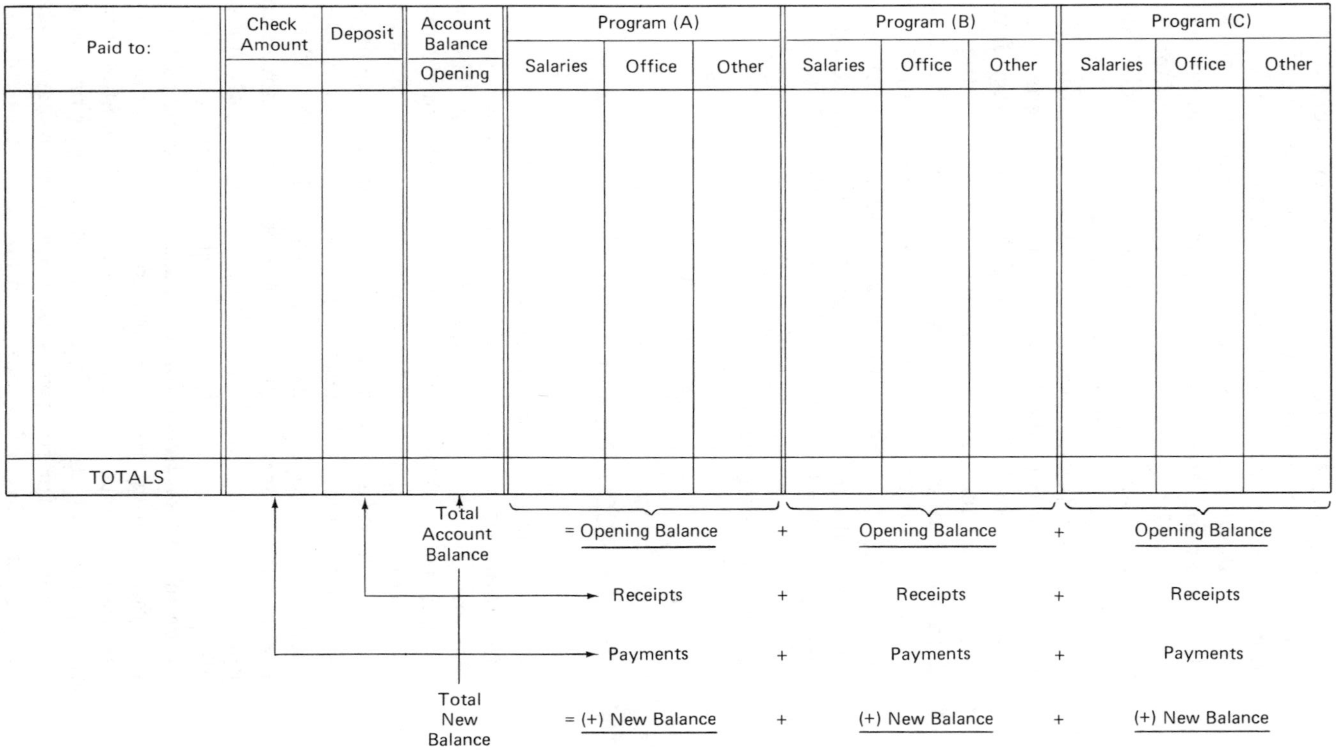

Paid to:	Check Amount	Deposit	Account Balance Opening	Program (A)			Program (B)			Program (C)		
				Salaries	Office	Other	Salaries	Office	Other	Salaries	Office	Other
TOTALS												

Total Account Balance = Opening Balance + Opening Balance + Opening Balance

Receipts → Receipts + Receipts + Receipts

Payments → Payments + Payments + Payments

Total New Balance = (+) New Balance + (+) New Balance + (+) New Balance + (+) New Balance

FIGURE 15. Explanation of a "fund balance" report (from the check register).

documentation—can be allayed. Consider Table 2 (page 35) as if there were three separately funded activities from different sources shown on Figure 15, Explanation of a Fund Balance Report. Budgets can be set up for any specific activity and their related expenditures tracked by a bookkeeping procedure. Fund balance reports should not be confused with "fund accounting," by which accountants formally categorize financial information in the statements of nonprofit organizations.

The modified accrual and the cash basis of accounting and reporting provide for a conservative statement of costs and revenues by including all unpaid bills and only funds actually received, rather than anticipated or owed to the organization. Even so, there are times when an additional comment to this regular report might be necessary. Any imminent but significant changes that for one reason or another would not be reflected in the report at the time it is presented should be noted by the manager. This added information will update and sometimes explain anomalies in a report or prepare the reviewers for sudden changes in the subsequent report.

THE INTERRELATIONSHIP OF MANAGEMENT AND THE ACCOUNTANT

The financial management function of budgeting is to plan for the utilization of resources in the future. Accounting is primarily concerned with what has happened in the past. The two activities meet in the continuous review responsibilities of the managers and governance participants. Internally, the accountant should be facilitating this review by designing information systems that will aid the decision makers. Accountants are facilitators of financial feedback as well as organizers of data collection. The review and re-evaluation concerns of the managers and the governance depend upon the quality of the reporting—timeliness, accuracy, and readability. The governance body must ask on a continuous basis if program targets, hence financial markers, are being met. The funding sources want to be assured on an independent basis through certified financial statements about how the money was spent, not on a daily basis but usually on a yearly basis or project basis.

The link for the two sets of decision makers is the measurement of the flow of resources in and out of the organization, the bills, the check register, and its subsidiary records (see Figure 16, "Financial Reporting").

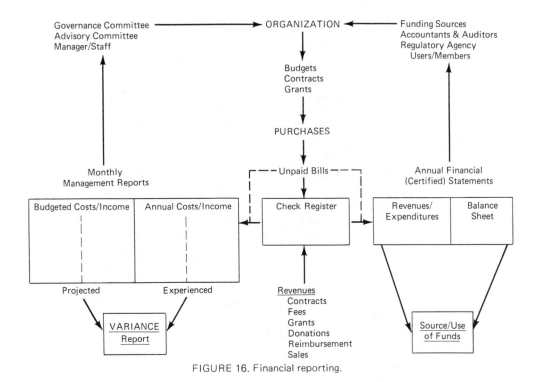

Governance Committee ⟶ ORGANIZATION ⟵ Funding Sources
Advisory Committee   Accountants & Auditors
Manager/Staff   Regulatory Agency
                                                Users/Members

Budgets
Contracts
Grants

PURCHASES

Monthly   ⌐ ─ ─ Unpaid Bills ─ ─ ┐   Annual Financial
Management Reports   (Certified) Statements

| Budgeted Costs/Income | Annual Costs/Income | Check Register | Revenues/Expenditures | Balance Sheet |

Projected   Experienced   Revenues   Source/Use
                                            Contracts   of Funds
VARIANCE   Fees
Report   Grants
                                            Donations
                                            Reimbursement
                                            Sales

FIGURE 16. Financial reporting.

THE VALUE OF
AUTOMATION TO MANAGEMENT

As previous pages of this book have shown, the financial numbers comprise the surface information of the activities in the organization. Arranging them and interpreting them for organizational control and planning purposes (feedback) is what financial reporting is all about. To relate the numbers with the people who are responsible for decision making is to maintain operating perspective and control. Consequently, any tendency to downgrade the financial information management tasks by seeing them purely as mechanical bookkeeping matters required by funding sources must be avoided. They are managerial responsibilities of the governance body. Their use by the latter and the managers contribute to successful operations.

As an organization grows, bookkeeping procedures can be developed and financial recording can be streamlined to enhance your ability to produce better financial information. This is clearly indicated in the application of "one-write" accounting systems that permit varied transactions to be recorded, organized, and made available for timely financial analysis and reporting.

Computerized payroll services are a valuable organizing tool commonly offered by banks and computer services companies or service bureaus across the nation. The mechanical work of recording payroll and issuing checks can be purchased at a reasonable price from these suppliers. Their services can provide comprehensive records of what is often the major cost and recordkeeping component of most activities in the nonprofit sector—wages, salaries, associated tax deductions, and fringe benefits. The key question to answer when you are considering the purchase of this type of recordkeeping service is, "Does the value of the bookkeeper's time spent on payroll accounting equal or surpass the cost of the comparable service?" The level at which costly bookkeeping time could be saved by substituting the service is related to the number of employees on the regular payroll and the frequency at which they are paid. If you only have a few people on the payroll, then this service is too costly. Weekly payrolls double the bookkeeping time of a biweekly payroll. So just paying every two weeks can reduce bookkeeping costs. In general, if you employ a minimum of twelve to fifteen employees it is worthwhile to sit down and make a few calculations about the administrative cost of the payroll preparation. Computerization of payroll recording does not eliminate the need for other bookkeeping tasks, nor making adjustments to payroll records. However, a lot of the tedious and error-producing work can be effectively transferred to a computerized program which will produce comprehensive records. Payroll verification must still be done by the organization and a formal authorization made to the business service or bank for issuance of payroll checks.

The cost to any particular organization is based on the number of computer runs and the volume of checks issued. Because a bank charges your organization for the total amount of the payroll checks issued in each pay period, you have to have that amount available in a special payroll account or in your regular account when the computer is run. That means there is little or no latitude for your organization in meeting salary payments on a timely basis.

The computerized report that accompanies each payroll run can be programmed to allocate personnel costs by project or contract, and show cumulative and current wage and salary payments. In this way information can be shaped for management reporting purposes as well as accounting records.

For small organizations, computerization of other financial information and monthly reporting often suffers from misapplication and misuse. After all, in most cases, it is not difficult to prepare a report of the financial transactions that are additional to regular payroll and to relate them to organizational activities and specific funding sources. The few computer-generated reports this author has seen do not appear to justify their expense. Employment of more elaborate data-processing reports is further confused by the fact that most nonfinancial participants who have to use or should be using such reports do not fully understand them as management tools. Automation tends to make financial reports more awesome to such readers. Because the data presentation is too often designed by accountants and program analysts for accounting purposes, the managerial format of the report is often confusing. Thus, even when electronic data-processing services may be appropriate and cost-effective, their bookkeeping value may be gained at the expense of not fulfilling the management information needs. Careful analysis and discussions with other users of data-processing systems must be undertaken before a decision is made about their use in small organizations. This is a task for all who are involved—board members, managers, and bookkeepers.

In sum, the financial information-gathering and reporting systems ultimately have to meet the needs of the managers and the organization's governance members. At the operational level, a calculation has to be made that will show that the purchase of a computerized data-processing service to replace the current methods of organizing bookkeeping tasks should provide a clear financial benefit. At the managerial and governance levels, either retraining of the users has to take place or the information must be presented so it can be understood by the average nonfinancial person using it to measure financial performance and position.

8

Cash-Flow Issues

Cash flow is the continuous difference between levels of cash coming into the project or organization and leaving it in the form of salaries, rent, phones, and other operating costs. Cash-flow difficulties arise from erratic flows of funds that cause an inability to meet essential and ongoing expenditures. This type of problem is not to be confused with spending more than a budget allows, or the common situation in which small organizations do not use some type of plan for expenditures related to anticipated income.

Take the example of your own salary and expenses. Every month you have to pay for your rent, telephone, and food bills—your "operating" costs. Like yourself, most people rely on a steady flow of income from their jobs to pay for these regularly occurring expenses. But assume that your income is erratic, even though you know what amount you will receive over a period of time, as long as you do your work. Given such conditions, you will probably have "cash-flow" problems from time to time. That is, in the absence of savings, you will not be able to pay for essential purchases or bills when you have to. This situation is very similar

106

to the financial experience of many small organizations that have reimbursement contracts for services which they produce. The gap between paying out funds for salaries, rent, utilities, and so forth and the arrival of the reimbursement check needs to be financed.

Situations of erratic flows of revenues characterize the financial management problems of profit-making organizations, as well as nonprofits. Expenses have to be paid, yet revenues do not come in time, nor as predicted. Unexpected expenditures have to be made or plans of activities redesigned and financed. Whatever the explanation, the highs and lows of revenue inflows and payments requirements do not coincide. Profit-making organizations that have to finance production or inventory of marketable goods before they can sell them have access to and are generally served by commercial banks. Through their business loans, such institutions assist in financing the cycles of resource purchases and resales. Nonprofits, especially small organizations, do not have this financing facility. Their reimbursement contracts often require them to pay for the resources they acquire and then bill the funding source. Rarely are advances provided for initial expenditures. Worse, and more important, the refunding "cycles" are often unpredictable, and revenues from them cannot be assumed to be available at specific times in the future to pay for new resource purchases or to repay a loan, if one could be obtained. Banks do not look at these operations as commercial situations, and consequently are hesitant to make loans to them unless they are personally guaranteed by people who can repay them.

FINANCIAL PLANNING

The financial planning for any program or organization not only answers the questions "How much do we need?" (functional budget projection) and "Where are the money or resources coming from?" (sources of funding); it also answers the question "When does the money come in from each source and go out for each resource?" (cash flow). The first two are budget and financial development concerns, the last is a cash management issue. Each has the same high level of importance to meeting your organization's present and future objectives. The following are major considerations in planning:

1. ANTICIPATE TOTAL COSTS
The main issue about getting programs started or rapidly expanding them is to adequately determine the amount of fi-

nancing necessary to initiate new activities and provide for
their continuous support. Lack of attention to the calculation of the costs of many new or added functions that are
necessary to carry out activities eventually produces a dismaying realization that there is not enough money to accomplish what you are trying to do. A common example occurs
when proposal writers leave out the costs of the bookkeeping
and an annual audited report prepared by a certified public
accountant. Either they have assumed that they will find a
volunteer accountant to do the services or they have not
given much thought to the financial administration of what
they plan to do. People who are not experienced in business
management often underestimate the cost and importance of
the various administrative functions necessary to their plan.
This is one of the most common causes of poor financial
planning of a project.

2. THE NEED FOR BUDGET FLEXIBILITY
While getting a project started on a "shoestring" budget is an
admirable entrepreneurial tradition, at some point of growth
payment will have to be made for many of your activities
for managerial and program functions. The one-person show
that got operations off the ground most likely entailed a 70-
hour-a-week job, the equivalent of two positions composed
of several major administrative and technical functions. A
large part of the start-up "cost" of the project was in fact contributed by a very spirited person or persons who provided
the needed resources. Recognition of all those functions and
estimating their future costs as part of the evolution of a
project is a subtle but important part of developing useful
financial projections and lasting activities. If you carefully
analyze activities, functions, and resource needs, with some
inputs from "financial" people whenever possible, you can
better anticipate the expenditures component of cash flow.

It is not unusual that certain program and administrative
needs are discovered only after a project is underway. Budgets only planned for minimal resource requirements are
drawn too tightly. They have no flexibility or built-in surplus
for variation or uncertainty. While you rarely are able to
obtain all the funding you think you need, project planning
should be for the ideal implementation, a slightly generous
but reasonable estimate of costs of needed functions. Minimum budgets have to be based on the possibility that things
don't go according to plan. For example, being prepared to
pay "up to" a certain amount for personnel and other resources is a more expansive and realistic approach to cost
estimating of personnel. Obtaining extra funds from another
source for your project as a reserve for contingencies, for

more marginal functions and resources, helps insure against the unpredictable expenditures that always seem to be necessary.

3. THE IMPACT OF FUNDING SOURCES

The type of financing you receive for your activities influences the financial problems your organization will experience and may highlight particular organizational functions that have to be performed for a successful venture. In the past, small nonprofit organizations creating public benefits were charity organizations. They were dependent on donations. But today, to a considerable and increasing extent, most of them "sell" services of one kind or another to federal, state, and local government agencies and private third-party payors such as insurance plans. Much of their funding is on a reimbursement basis. Such arrangements mean that they purchase resources, develop and provide services, then seek reimbursement for the obligations incurred in accordance with predetermined contractual agreements. In general, the financial conditions of such contracts are that the provider organization must arrange initial financing, and that continual financing is dependent on the review of expenditures and refunding cycle of the contracting organization.

The risks of repayment and delayed payment are borne by the provider organization! Sometimes, there are provisions (such as advances or credit arrangements) in contractual agreements which recognize the financing limitations of the small organization. But generally, refunding arrangements are designed in terms of the control, convenience, and even inefficiency of the funding sources. As a result, many human service agencies often find their financing tied to the inconsistencies of poorly administered contracts. Under that circumstance, financial planning of the small agency must take into account the financing procedures and possible unreliability of the funding sources that affect the income component of an organization's cash flow.

The implementation of every new activity or contract will have financial impact on the organization's pattern of financial flows, given the refunding procedures and consistency of management of the contracting agency. How the new financing patterns will effect the overall flow must be determined and planned far in advance, either in the contract negotiations or through the development of some other financial capability such as contingency funds, cash reserves, loans, supplier credits, special fund-raising events, and so forth.

PROJECTING CASH FLOW

The general starting point for making a simple cash-flow projection of any activity program or business is to ask yourself what your financial needs are for a given period based on specific purchases of resources, and when these needs will have to be paid for. Office space, telephone, some furniture, a typewriter (rent or buy), stationery, and legal assistance are some of the essential resources needed for getting any kind of activity underway. While it is true that you or someone may contribute the costs of these resources in kind or by personal efforts, sooner or later these and other expenses may have to be paid for in cash. So make a list similar to the one in the start-up budget of Table 4. Give it a time framework. Make it in enough detail so that you will carefully think about the necessary expenditures of your undertaking. Then consider when you can expect income to flow into your organization, either based on prior commitments—grants, contracts, dues, sales, and so on—or what you might have to do (marketing and grantsmanship) to generate such funds. From juxtaposing the expected income and the outgo of cash, you can then see expected cash needs in advance. Suppose you plan to put on a conference for a special audience. After determining what you will do, you make the cash-flow projection illustrated in Table 6.

TABLE 6. Cash-flow Projection

Month:	1	2	3	4	5	6
Costs Outflow						
Personnel	$ —	$ —	$ —	$ —	$ —	$ 60
Office	—	—	150	150	150	150
Telephone	—	—	50	60	60	60
Office Supplies	20	10	10	10	20	10
Postage	10	20	30	30	30	20
Furniture/Typewriter (rent)	—	40	40	40	40	40
Exhibit/Conference					250	400
Total	$30	$70	$280	$290	$550	$ 740
Inflow Sources						
$ Contributions	$10	$ 50	$100	$ —	$ —	$ —
Dues/Fees	—	20	120	200	150	400
Grants		100	—			800
Donated Skills/Resources	x	x	x	x	x	x
	$10	$170	$220	$200	$150	$1200
Net Cash Surplus/(Deficit)	-($20)	$100	-($60)	-($90)	-($400)	$ 460
Cumulative		80	20	-($70)	-($470)	-($10)

110

TABLE 7. Cash-flow Plan from Figure 5

				MONTH			
	0	1	2	3	4	5	
Expenditures							
A. Current Month		$1,350	$3,648	$6,054	$7,000	$7,000	
B. Cumulative		$1,350	$4,998	$11,052	$18,052	$25,052	
Revenues							
C. Voucher		First		$1,350	$3,648	$6,054	$7,000
D. Cumulative		Request		$1,350	$4,998	$11,052	$18,052
Cash-Flow Difference (B–D)							
Net to be financed due to reimbursement lag time			$4,998	$9,702	$13,054	$14,000	

As with all plans, these are projections. But cash-flow projections are also financial objectives, or markers, for you. They have to be reviewed and reassessed continually, and certainly, if money is borrowed against them, someone else may want to review them carefully.

Since reimbursement funding is a typical financing mechanism in the private nonprofit sector, let us look at the start-up budget of the Child Abuse Program. Figure 5 (page 50), seen in terms of a cash outflow calculation, can incorporate a reimbursement cycle. Inflow of revenues is based on (1) a time lag between the period in which the expenditures are made and presented in a bill to the funding source (reimbursement voucher) and (2) the processing time of the funding source. Assuming a 30- to 40-day processing cycle following submission of reimbursement requests (vouchers) at the end of each month, the financial projection illustrated in Table 7 could be anticipated.

This chart shows that the total time lag—the period during which expenditures are made, vouchered, and finally reimbursed— may be more than two months. Thus by the end of the second month $4,998 has been spent and the reimbursement from the first month has not arrived. The third month's expenditures are $6,054, so cumulative expenses are $11,052. But the first reimbursement arrived so the net financing needs to that point are $9,702. At full operation, as least two months' expenses will always be outstanding before the next reimbursement check arrives.

It is possible that some of this amount can be financed through suppliers, especially if you explain your relationship with the funding source(s) and the expected time you will receive reimbursement to be able to make payments. Of course, there are two underlying assumptions for the above calculation: (1) that your organization promptly sends an accurate reimbursement voucher, and (2) that you can count on a 30- to 40-day processing mechanism of the funding source. The latter may be a questionable assumption about many government agencies.

Technically, a "reimbursement" cycle in fact takes place anytime that goods and services are acquired for cash or an obligation (a credit) that is subsequently reconverted into cash. It makes no difference in a financial sense if the final source of cash is a reimbursement contract or an actual sale. What is important is that different activities and funding sources create different cycles of cash flow for an organization. Not only does the cash-flow "gap" between purchases of resources and the receipt of proceeds from the "resale" (in one form or another) of the final products have to be financed; there is also the possibility that the resale or reimbursement is not made within an expected time framework, or not made at a price that fully recovers the cost of resources used in production. Of course when some form of reimbursement does not occur at all, the purchaser still has to pay for the resources that were acquired. The use and resale of the output of the resources and skills is the organization's risk, not that of the vendor.

Conditions of funding and reimbursement vary with each source and type of contractual arrangement. Accordingly, calculations should be made for the flows of funds for each project. Add all the projects' flows together and you have a projected cash flow for the organizations' activities. In ongoing organizations, it is important that managers and board members look in detail at and plan for the possible effects of negative cash-flow changes in their operations when new projects are being considered. In order to avoid the usual financial "crunch" caused by rapidly growing expenditures and delays in receipts of reimbursement, some type of financing of the cash-flow "gap" has to be considered. Two factors are extremely important in looking at the problems of cash-flow projections:

1. You should clarify expectations about reimbursement payments, billing, and financial reporting with the funding source. If possible, verify these with other grantees or contractors to realistically determine time lags and problems you may experience. If you are engaged in a business enterprise, there are some common conditions and commercial practices that will affect and define the financial flows of your particular trade. They are usually not a mystery.

2. Think carefully about which management functions will be required of your organization to be involved in any funding processes. In fact, whatever the financing mechanism indicated—public fund-raising, grants and contracts, fees, insurance reimbursements, monthly dues, sales, and so forth—the careful analysis and planning of different management support for contracts administration, marketing, advertising, fund raising, grants developing, bookkeeping, and accounting is essential. The solvency and long-term impact of your organization may depend on attention to and investment in these functions.

If you are able to control expenditures and maintain an operating schedule, and if the project records and bills are submitted in an orderly, accurate, and timely manner, there is still no assurance that outside funding and refunding is necessarily predictable, even with binding contracts. Your organization has done its part to manage resources. The fact is that you may be dependent on funding mechanisms over which you probably have little influence. If that is your situation, then it is important for your organization to try to diversify its activities and funding sources in such a way as to create different flows of payments and income.

WHAT TO DO ABOUT CASH GAPS

How do you pay for resources you need to acquire before reimbursement and other revenues are generated? There are many possibilities—volunteer work, personal contributions and loans, start-up grants and loans, vendors' credits, membership fees, dues, deposits, and the like. Advances are available under some types of funding agreements. Many federal government grants and contracts provide for advanced funding arranged on a basis of periodic requests for estimated cash needs of the coming months. However, federal funds have been increasingly going to and through state agencies to be managed on a subgrantee and subcontract level. As a consequence, financial procedures are set by state agencies. They are guided by state laws and administrative mechanisms, which usually eliminate advanced funding and require reimbursement procedures. This change greatly magnifies the financial planning problems of small organizations.

Banks generally do not consider the reimbursement voucher a commercial obligation against which they can safely secure or relate a short-term loan. Though the voucher is in fact a bill to the originial contracting agency, it is not a promise to pay on the part of that agency. It must be accepted by the funding source in the same way that you approved your vendors' bills before authorizing payment. When a funding source has a poor reputation for meeting its contractual obligations and managing its own payment procedures, even a perfectly acceptable voucher is not very useful for banking considerations.

As a practical matter, there are many factors that may cause a breakdown in voucher approval and payment procedures of a reimbursing source. Even though a funding agency may share the same concern in word and deed that you feel about the importance of implementing your project, don't count on an orderly refunding procedure as part of your financial plan. Assume the worst possible funding conditions when making a cash-flow projection. Yes, admittedly the foregoing cash-flow plan of the first five months of the Child Abuse Program is idealistic; it is not based on the "worst possible conditions." But at least the assumptions are clear about when revenues are expected to flow from the reimbursing agency. You and a governance committee should evaluate the cash-flow assumptions of your activities in your overall financial planning, as well as in individual undertakings.

On the other hand, start-up managers, staff, and others involved in developing small nonprofit organizations may be dealing with reimbursement mechanism for the first time. To be frank, they often do not have the slightest idea of what they should do even when common sense is an appropriate guide. Many managers simply do not want to deal with finances or are afraid of them. But in order not to create unnecessary problems in funding and refunding processes, it is essential that the manager take full responsibility for understanding what has to be done.

Since timely submission of voucher data in accordance with requirements of the funding source helps eliminate potential refunding problems, a top priority of the financial manager is to see that the reimbursement voucher is carefully prepared each month or whenever it is due. A meeting with funding representatives a week or two before the paperwork initially begins will be helpful in getting procedural details straightened out. If an assistant is going to carry out the billing procedure in your organization, he or she should be at this meeting to learn the details firsthand and meet the people in the agency. Since reimbursement is often an important financial lifeline of an organization, at least two staff members should know how it is done and who to contact at the funding sources. There is nothing more important in the financial management role than to ensure that the organization's part of the reimbursement process is carried out effectively.

The budget projection of Table 2 (page 35) shows the levels of obligations incurred each month. The amount of cash needed is not necessarily the same or proportional. That depends on the types of obligations that your organization incurs and when they are due. Salaries and fringe benefits such as health insurance have to be paid currently for legal reasons and organizational morale. Different payroll related taxes have different schedules. Occasionally you might be able to be a few days late with salaries, as long as everyone shares the sacrifice, fully understands the delay, and agrees to it. But remember that you have a contract with your employees which states or implies that they will be paid on a regular basis. Beyond the dry conditions of a contract, it is the organizational dynamics that are undermined when staff members are worried about getting paid while they are trying to meet program expectations or provide services to those in need. So it is important to always try to have the next payroll in the bank as the minimum balance in the checkbook while you authorize payment of other bills.

Each vendor has financial constraints built into the prices and terms of sale of goods and services to you. Paid staff have certain financial constraints which they expect to be met and responded to in their salary and wage agreements. The telephone company is not in the business of financing its consumers, thus it requires a relatively short period for making payments. Other vendors vary as to the time they will expect to receive payment for whatever they have provided you. Some suppliers even offer discounts for early payment of their bills. They pass the savings of their financing costs on to you through this mechanism. With many vendors you can often obtain 30-day credit or be billed at the end of the month rather than pay in cash. Thus vendor credits can temporarily finance your purchase of resources. Vendors are interested in your business, because if you grow they often have the prospect of selling more to you. Tell them what you do; enlist them in your cause! Sometimes vendors can work with you by extending credit on more than their normal terms and by making arrangement for partial payment. These arrangements may help to ease your needs for cash on hand. In many instances, their interests are not just "business as usual." Local businesspeople participate by bending their own rules because of the importance of your efforts. But vendors are suppliers of resources and skills that have to be paid for if they are going to be available to your organization in the future.

115

Many vendors who deal with small nonprofits are wary about nonpayment of bills. Suppose a consumers' information and advocacy group is partially funded by foundation money and also relies on public contributions to meet its annual operating costs. The level of the latter part of the funding is uncertain. The risks to the vendor of office supplies and printing services are not simply "when" funds will be available for bills, but also "if" enough funds will be raised.

There are some people who reason that not paying bills of vendors who are large "anonymous" corporations is somehow justifiable. After all, "They can afford it" or "They rip us off anyhow." Vendors, large or small, are still accountable for losses in credit sales. Your organization—specifically, the officers and board members—is legally accountable for its obligations. As a practical matter, the representative of the large vendor, who you may have convinced to extend credit, is very directly responsible for your actions of slow or no payment. He or she is not anonymous. That person's judgment and reliability may have been jeopardized by your actions. So who can afford it? Your acts define your organization's commercial reputation. They also define the attitude of those (your board or constituency) who trusted you to carry out the goals of the organization.

If you have made promises to pay a vendor and subsequently find that revenues have not come into your organization as anticipated, it is better to talk directly with the seller than to send a "rubber" check, or not to respond. If you have not initially misled the vendor, you can often explain your financial situation and work together on meeting your obligations. Of course, too many stories and excuses are self-defeating. You will soon have a deservedly poor reputation for not paying your bills and will not be offered the credit of vendors to finance your activities. Then your purchases will require cash "up front." Your general ability to pay bills will deteriorate, because vendors will require cash before you use and sell the benefits of these resources.

In sum, an important financial objective in managing the payment of your obligations is to try to schedule vendor credits to coincide with the flows of funds into your organization. Thus the amount of currently due unpaid bills will be minimized. This is particularly useful if the bulk of your funding is under reimbursement contracts. But in general, it is a basic financial management principle for any operation, profit or nonprofit.

IV

ECONOMIC
ENTERPRISES

9

The Not-for-Profit
Business Enterprise

BUSINESS ENTERPRISES:
PROFIT OR NONPROFIT?

One way to look at the purposes or goals of any new activity, whether it is a traditional business enterprise or a nonprofit service organization, is in terms of channeling resources productively into new ways of meeting society's needs. "Enterprise" here refers to meeting communal needs in new ways, on a commercial basis, not whether the activities are labeled as profit-making, private, public, or private nonprofit. Most of the founders of major corporations started with this perspective of innovation, as did many government undertakings such as the Tennessee Valley Authority, the Bay Area Rapid Transit Corporation (subway system between Berkeley and San Francisco), and private, nonprofit activities such as rural electric cooperatives, mutually owned savings and loan associations, credit unions, and farm supplies cooperatives.

Of course all of us can point to questionable uses of resources that satisfied presumed "needs" of society as measured by conventional marketplace criteria. A few years ago some consumers made the "pet rock," an adult toy, a surprising success in financial and marketing terms. But consumers also rejected the ill-conceived "Edsel" model Ford in the early fifties. It was a dramatic and costly failure in its time. Somewhere in the middle of these extreme examples lies most of our attempts to effectively convert our ideas into fulfilling what we think are needed products and services. Correspondingly, we are also consumers, who can and do make choices about what we want and what we will pay to fulfill our "needs," real or illusory.

Nonprofit organizations that provide human services under "purchase of service" agreements with and grants from government agencies, or that provide public service activities supported by private sources (foundations, corporations, churches, and individuals), are not concerned with the question of whether the consumer or the client will pay for the proposed service. Most of their support is based on the presumption that the group in need or "market" they would benefit cannot pay at all. With other services such as orchestras and museums, for which the cost of the services or products is greater than can be reasonably paid by many of the consumers, public support usually makes up the difference between the public "value" (benefits) and the user charges. The focus of management of nonprofit organizations providing human services is on the development and delivery of their services as inexpensively as possible, and arranging funding from the public and private sources. They compete among themselves on a program as well as a cost basis for available funding. More often than not, this funding is sought and secured prior to project implementation. Consumer or client acceptance of the services is not in marketplace terms of prices or "fee for services" rendered. Since fees reflecting costs would not be affordable by the desired user, they are not a condition of support by funding sources.

The alcohol abuser, particularly among the lower income groups, cannot afford medical and other services available in the "fee for service" (commercial) market to meet his or her needs, whereas those with money can. Pricing of various alcohol services, if done at all, may be on a sliding scale basis, according to the ability of the user to pay rather than the cost of production. This holds true for many other public activities as well as social services. The simple mechanism of charging a special or students' price for museum entry is a recognition that user price cannot be based on cost. Thus public support and the "ability to pay" criteria weigh the benefits of a service or activity in terms of the public/user well-being rather than market price based on costs to produce it. The value of the output, not always easily measurable, is reasoned by the delivery agency and the funding sources to be greater than the costs of production, especially when volunteer and in-kind contributions are utilized. Thus in the nonprofit sector, a nontraditional market mechanism of pricing is established by provider organizations and funding sources rather than between consumers and providers. Illustrative of such activities are public mental health services, drug and alcohol addiction prevention and treatment programs, foster care, services for the elderly, and public issues and education activities such as saving endangered wildlife. Many cultural and fine arts programs are partially supported by user fees essentially based on ability to pay. In effect, funding sources, when they are subsidizing or fully supporting the costs of the activities, act for and in the marketplace of the consuming public. They are funding a public option for those unable to pay. Innovation is the source of the option.

To look at public and private sources of funds as investors is to emphasize that they are financing change in how resources are used to meet ever changing needs in the society, rather than "giving" money away or even "making grants" to good causes. They are, in this interpretation, accepting the risks of (1) the validity or usefulness of a nonprofit activity and (2) the possibility of poor management of resources. These separable elements of risk reflect program and managerial components of any organized effort. However, the benefits derived from overcoming these risks and producing a successful project do not accrue to the investors as they normally would in the private sector. Successful projects directly benefit the general and specific publics and indirectly validate the economic and political utility of the funding sources. When projects do not work out, sources incur financial "losses" in the form of wasted resources and even poor reputations. Such losses are a cost of innovation, of "research and development" in the public sector. They are the equivalent of losses generated along with benefits of innovative activity found among the private profit-making organizations.

RISK AND FEASIBILITY OF NOT-FOR-PROFIT BUSINESSES

The term "not for profit" is here used to refer to business or commercial enterprises in the private nonprofit sector. While those who develop and promote such enterprises may not be concerned with generating profits for themselves, they do operate in a competitive and commercial environment that relates costs of their activities with the satisfaction of consumer/user needs. In this respect, they are no different from any private profit-seeking organization. Thus in any discussion of commercial activities, our conceptual framework must shift to considerations of marketing and sales, because the buyer has the ultimate say as to whether a product meets his or her needs. Generally, if a project cannot be managed and financed to produce something better and cheaper than what is available, it is not likely to be economically or organizationally viable. Whether or not something is indeed "better and cheaper" is a decision made by the purchaser. Very simplistically, the purchaser votes. That vote means the validation of meeting someone's needs, and thereby the continuance of the business by payment for its production.

As noted earlier, risk is the possibility that our attempts to meet a need may not be "successful" as we and others expect. An idea may not have been commercially "feasible" in the first place, or conditions may have changed subsequent to your conceiving it. Assessing the feasibility of a business project has to do with various practical questions about translating an idea into action. As in Chapter Three, the strategy and activities of any project should initially be weighed and planned, but there is a new emphasis on commercial relationships with users/consumers and commercial financial sources. Thus project formulation guidelines of Chapter Three must be reshaped to answer the following questions:

1. *PRICE TRANSLATION OF COST OF OUTPUT*
   Is there an adequate estimate of what the project will cost, and a determination that the benefits to the users, in terms of pricing of the outputs, will be equal to or greater than the costs to produce them? Does the project assume a very high proportion of volunteer investment? What is their expected compensation?

2. *MARKET ACCEPTANCE*
   Is there a possibility that the final product will not be accepted by the consumer? Will there be enough consumers who will pay for the full costs of production?

3. *TECHNICAL AND MANAGEMENT SKILLS*
   Are the technical and managerial skills available to make the best use of resources for the project—i.e., to operate it efficiently or productively?

4. *MAJOR BUSINESS FACTOR CHANGES*
   Is there a likelihood of change in the technology, marketing, finance, or even legal conditions in the near future that may invalidate the purpose and strategy of this project?

Before any other aspects of planning a business venture are analyzed, you should seriously consider how the purpose of an activity can be better served by a cooperative or a not-for-profit enterprise rather than a profit-making organization. After all, a profit-making organization does not have to make a large profit, and neither type can lose money for too long and still remain operative in responding to a need. Insofar as a profit is made in doing so, a financial reward is generated for the risk that the owners financed. But there are other rewards derived from solving problems and meeting needs in the society. A not-for-profit enterprise will pay taxes on its surplus earnings just like any other commercial enterprise. In terms of the commercial environment, our economy is highly mixed and flexible. Many new enterprises form and die every day. The components of risk are the same for everyone. While capital is not free, it is not scarce. Political and economic controls are minimal in our society, so

1. What is to be gained by being organized as a not-for-profit enterprise in terms of goals and strategy?
2. Can you obtain the benefits elsewhere, from some other organization even though the price/cost is higher?
3. What are the human requirements that would be served other than the legal, ideological ones?
4. Is the cooperative effort "for them" (an external need or market) or for yourselves?
5. What are the practical managerial and investment decision implications that this type of organization presents?
6. Are the benefits temporary or lasting?

Popular ideas, people's needs, and the real costs of organizing and operating any enterprise can easily be confused with one another and not carefully evaluated. Should our cooperative sawmill sell firewood in the city for less than other businesses do, or is our purpose limited to supplying the needs of our rural members? Would you join a natural foods co-op that would require its members to work for two or three hours a month in order to buy products at 25 percent less than the price of alternative suppliers? Will cooperative housing for the elderly support lower rents and be a means whereby needed community facilities can be organized? Such questions have a lot to do with "why" and "how" your organization operates, all of which can be translated into costs and benefits.

Investors are usually associated with profit-making activities, but in the larger sense of their role, they are people and organizations that support the undertaking of risks of using resources in new ways for new benefits, either societal or personal. Benefits of new utilization of resources may also substantially accrue to workers—more and better paying jobs; to consumers—useful products and services; to managers—challenging use of skills; to creditors—productive channeling of funds. The investor is the person or group to whom/which both profits and losses accrue, depending on whether the business idea turns out to be commercially feasible or not. Employees sell their skills for fixed returns. There is considerable legal and insurance protection for them in the sale of their services. Commercial banks sell the use of money in the form of loans. Because they have bought the use of other people's money and are subject to strict rules about how they can invest their resources, they are usually very careful about how they re-employ their funds. They take bankers' risks. Most of their lending is secured by the assets for which it is used or by other assets of the borrower. Their primary job is to lend on a short-term basis, less than one year, to finance the cycle of production, or wholesale purchase of goods and services, for resale. Long-term lenders finance resources used in production, such as equipment and buildings. The owners take the greater risk in the long-term mobilization of resources. They undertake the financial risk that others will not. The risks of the enterprise, marketable products and the capable management, are the same whether you buy shares in a cooperative or General Motors Corporation.

NOT-FOR-PROFIT OWNERSHIP

Given the perspective of this book, it is important to distinguish between profit-making activities that are cooperatively and collectively operated for the benefit of a relatively few owners and those that are run for the benefit of consumers who are also owners. The former, such as "worker-owned" businesses or producer cooperatives, are profit-making enterprises for their owners. The worker-owners may make collective decisions about policy and practice or may establish a strictly hierarchical managerial structure of paid, non–owner managers to operate their business. How decisions are made is a matter of organizational philosophy. The end result is to produce a profit for them as owners and to avoid risk of losses of their investment as much as possible. Ownership and consumption of the product or service are among separate publics. In addition to being owners, they may also sell other resources to the same enterprise and thereby receive salaries and wages from employment of skills, lend money, and receive interest.

In Oregon and Washington there are a number of worker-owned plywood factories. They are cooperatively operated in a very competitive and cyclical industry. The workers are the sole owners. They sell their products in the same market channels as other plywood companies. They compete for the same national market with a standardized product. Each worker owns a share and has a vote in the control of the operating policy and management decisions of his company. The shares have financial value representing assets and earning power of the companies. They are transferable at a significant price to new workers. The profit from business ventures is taken out in wages that are much higher than the local industry normally pays for the same skills of its non-owner workers. Of course when business is not good, there may be times when wages are lower, by comparison with other companies. Thus their wages reflect the owners' risk as well as a sale of productive skills. Owners' risk translates to potential benefits from the profitability of the enterprise and the possible burden of losses. Even though their organizational structure is very different from other plywood companies, they are traditional capitalists, since maximization of benefits for the owners is their major goal.

Now consider a consumer food cooperative in which a large number of individual users are owner-members. They have rights and responsibilities as members, and as owners. They seek to benefit as consumers from lower food prices, availability of special products, quality, and the like. Generally, they are open to whoever wants to join. Some of the members may be paid staff with health insurance and vacation time, fringe benefits that may have been considered to be an important employment compensation. Other members may be participants in some type of governance structure, a board of trustees or a policy-making committee designed to represent the membership at large, or a small working group with a particular task. Their decisions or recommendations are generally intended to benefit all the members. Indeed, decision making is carried out in the name of member/consumers, who are the member/owners. As a group they have taken on the risk that the cooperative will not be able to produce the benefits that they expect.

It is these types of owner/user–oriented, not-for-profit businesses that are referred to hereafter.

IMPLICATIONS OF SUBSIDIES TO
AND GENERAL FEASIBILITY OF
BUSINESSES

A cooperative enterprise is an economically competitive business activity. Its promoters and supporters must look at the business and finance of a commercial venture, as well as the organizational structure and governance issues of cooperative decision making. Though not for profit, such enterprises are not tax-exempt, since their primary purpose is of a business nature. Commercially, their business costs and credit availability will reflect the riskiness others perceive about the purpose of the business activity and management of the enterprise.

Many organizational functions and much productive equipment may have to be financed long before they generate enough returns to pay their way. Some commercial financing through supplier credits may be available, but for most new enterprises, it is not easy to obtain. Banks cannot lend to such operations since the risk of repayment is so great. These conditions reflect the business risks of creditors in dealing with new eneterprises. To reduce risk, members of cooperatives can contribute the value of many of the needed resources in the form of their skills, goods, and services in kind, cash contributions, fees, and share purchases, or other financial arrangements. Financing, when not expected to be repaid, for the owners' equity or capital. Contributed skills and assets as "necessary" functions and productive equipment have a cash or market value, hence an owners' value. There is in fact an economic exchange taking place when such contributions are made. Sooner or later the values of these contributions have to be accounted for in order to adequately price the output if the enterprise is to provide anticipated benefits to its users and continue to operate at a level at which costs are met.

The idea of adequate pricing involves the eventual recognition of the full costs of production, regardless of the fact they are paid in cash or may be donated skills or subsidized financing. "Free" skills that are necessary to a project have a distinct and calculable value in the total cost of the output of an enterprise. Most people who donate such skills expect something in return. If the benefits do not materialize, or more important, do not measure up to their expectations, the donors tend to withdraw their "free" resources. When skills are paid for, the wage becomes the primary expectation in the exchange of resources, rather than the outcome of a project. If an enterprise depends on a high level of volunteer labor in order to create user benefits, then the reasons for motivating such contribution usually have to have concrete value. Where this is an important source of financing, organizers and managers have to assume that a worthwhile exchange takes place. To assume that because "we are cooperative and nonprofit" is an adequate exchange for people's resources and creativity is to not value their importance nor understand that there is an economic contract being made, however implicit.

To have a subsidy essentially means that someone else has taken part of the commercial risk of financing the enterprise and will absorb part of the cost of failure of the project. If the feasibility of a project is dependent upon the subsidy of outside organizations, then the benefits of the project usually in some way support the goals and objectives of the subsidizers. Thus there are industry subsidies from federal government agencies for training "hard-core" unemployed, and subsidized financing from economic development corporations which support job-producing business projects. There is subsidized financing of managerial resources to new and growing cooperatives through technical assistance provided by the National Consumers Cooperative Bank, which is separate from any loan commitment. Perhaps the most commonly known and utilized source of subsidized personnel resources in the nonprofit sector was the CETA program of the Department of Labor. CETA has been sharply curtailed since 1980. Through its programs, large numbers of unemployed people have the potential of being retrained and developing new skills while working for private nonprofit organizations, as well as in the public and the private sectors.

Development financing is different from commercial financing in that its financial terms are designed to reduce the risks and widen the availability of capital to new or rapidly growing organizations. A bank loan generally is not development financing, since the business risks of the latter are normally too high. But as a business grows and proves itself to be a viable operating entity it has greater access to more commercial capital. In the private sector, venture capital for new and high-risk enterprises requires the potential of high rewards for its use. Investments are often structured through purchase of a significant portion of the ownership or loans convertible into an ownership interest. The public, through government agencies and nonprofit organizations, also takes risks of providing financial assistance to business situations that do not qualify for normal commercial terms but have good prospects of economic success and expansion of employment. This is typically done through community development corporations, state economic development and financing programs, and the

Small Business Administration (SBA). Though some of their capital is available for new ventures, they typically make low-interest long-term development loans after many of the start-up risks of a new enterprise have been reduced, and owners have invested some capital. They subsidize growth that other investors and creditors generally will not undertake. The major program of SBA is the guarantee of bank loans to growing companies.

The usual expectancy in most if not all development financing is that at some point an enterprise will reach a level of commercial risk in the competitive marketplace which can be financed by unsubsidized capital. The enterprise will then be economically feasible. Various commercial sources of funding available to all businesses—suppliers' credit, short-term bank loans for inventories and credit sales, longer-term loans for equipment and mortgages for buildings, and new owners' investment—will be more available at that stage of the business development.

The financial problem addressed in development financing is for an operation to have enough funds to support the growth of its activities until revenues can cover costs, or meet commercial financing requirements to attract other resource suppliers. Development funding objectives are to substitute scarce and expensive capital in high-risk projects for reasonable terms, which encourages other investors to participate. A financial subsidy essentially absorbs some part of the risk of the enterprise and thereby reduces the remaining risk among other suppliers of credit and resources. It makes a project self-sustaining or financially feasible earlier in its life than if it were subject to fully meeting commercial conditions. However, if the investment risks are not met the component of development financing will be subject to relatively greater loss than other investors.

THE CHALLENGE OF
COOPERATIVE ENTERPRISE

The fact that the consumer/user may also be an owner of the enterprise adds another dimension to the complexity of financial and managerial issues, as objectives of "cheaper and better" are translated into organization policy and business expectations. A consumer co-op member is in a unique position to learn about both sides of a business decision in a way that is rarely possible in another part of the private business sector. As a practical matter, the active co-op member must know more about his or her business because of this unique situation of owner and user concerns (costs and expectations) merging in decision-making activities. The market and the consumer are not "out there," as in the usual situation of a profit-making enterprise. It may be possible to have much better communication about the needs to be fulfilled and the organizational costs to fulfill them than usually exists in most private enterprise. Thus cooperative benefits can be outstanding because of the potential unity of owner/consumer interests and informed decision making. But the losses can be dismaying owing to unresolved conflicts from lack of understanding of managerial needs and business perspective, unclear assumptions about general purposes, and specific objectives of the organization. The uniqueness of this type of member organization indicates an unusual aspect of business management risk.

Just because you have a cooperative, not-for-profit enterprise does not mean that people will automatically join your efforts. If they do join, there is no guarantee that they will make full use of or buy the products that the enterprise produces. The cooperative as a competitive business, as an innovating organization responding to economic and financial needs of its members, has to develop and maintain its organizational and financial credibility both within for its members and without in order to utilize commercial financial sources. It has to create consumer/user satisfaction for its products and services. That requires various marketing functions and management orientation that include dealing extensively with diverse parts of the business community and sometimes government, as well as the consumers. Business and financial planning is greatly aided by having some knowledge of the particular business, as well as the energy and financing of people who are involved in the enterprise.

10

The Financing of Production

Regardless of the managerial format and the distribution of ownership, the feasibility of a business project depends on organizing resources productively to meet the anticipated needs of customers/users. In relation to pricing of output, if the end products or services are priced at a level that fully reflects the costs of their production, and the potential purchasers are willing to pay that price, then a business venture has a strong basis for survival and it may even flourish. The financial framework of all business activities (Figure 17A, "The Flow of Financing") essentially shows that categories of sources, generally owners and lenders (creditors), provide money to finance the purchase of resources (assets) and human skills used to produce services and products. As output is sold, resources that have been used up are reconverted into cash. Funds are available to cover the costs of production, including interest, and repay the principal of loans to creditors. If there is a surplus over costs, the owners may receive a distribution of it.

130

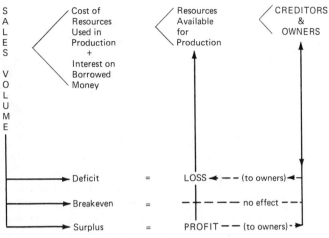

FIGURE 17A. Flow of financing.

Given a price limit in a competitive environment, a certain volume of production and sales is needed by an enterprise to pay its way. There is a minimum level of sales that will cover all costs of production, including replacement of equipment. At that level, an enterprise can be financially self-sufficient.

Price and volume are critical, interrelated determinants of project feasibility. Prices have to reflect costs of your activities, but at the same time they are subject to what potential buyers are willing to pay. Most often as you sell more output, your costs to produce a dollar's worth of sales falls, because some costs such as salaries, rent, and other general (indirect) costs can be divided by more and more units or volume of sales. In a competitive environment the level of sales that will produce enough income to cover all costs of production is called the "breakeven" volume. It is the minimum level toward which any manager must strive to operate an enterprise so it will not lose money invested by its sources of financing.

Since an enterprise is a structure for redirecting the use of resources in an economy, the financing sources bear the risk of whether adequate sales volume can be achieved with the new utilization of resources, and whether the valuation of the output through market pricing is what the consumer/purchaser is willing to pay. If the level of income from sales is less than the total costs of production during a given period, the financial sources have to make up the difference—the "loss"—in one form or another. The owners bear the risk of not recovering the costs of resources used up, since repayments to creditors are legal obliga-

131

tions unrelated to how effectively they have employed borrowed funds in their business. Ownership capital from the sales of shares, rights, fees, and even donated labor is a source of owners' financing, hence absorption of losses. If losses continue, sooner or later creditors will not lend and other investors will quit providing funds or their substitute. The business will collapse. On the bright side, if revenues surpass the costs of production, a surplus will arise. It can be redistributed as "dividends" to owners or an actual cash rebate to users. Lower prices can be charged to purchasers. The funds could also be reinvested in the enterprise in the form of adding assets for expansion, replacing old equipment, or reducing debts. Surplus could be used to pay bonuses, increase wages, and create a reserve for unexpected expenditures. The owners have the prerogative of choosing how to use the surplus, since it is the reward to them for overcoming risks of developing a feasible business operation. Thus the calculation and monitoring of production costs is critical to setting prices and promoting sales. The formal summaries of these financial transactions of costs of production, revenues, changes in levels of resources (assets) employed, and their financing (liabilities) from lenders, and shareholders' or owners' capital, compose the common accounting reports (the profit and loss statement and the balance sheet) of all enterprises.

Looking at Figure 17B, "Income, Costs, Resources, and Financing," the *balance sheet* shows how the financing by owners and lenders (creditors) has been utilized to acquire different types of assets needed in the production and sales of the goods and services that are the output of the organization. It is a measurement of available resources and their financing at any given time. As resources are used up and sold, their costs are reduced from the assets, and shown on the income statement.

The *profit and loss statement*, often called the income statement, is an accounting of the revenues from the sales during a given period of time and the costs of the specific amount of labor and materials used in the production or inventory that was sold. It is a periodic financial measure of the amount of resources "used up" in the output that was sold, and the dollar amount received from sales. The reduction is shown in the latter as general categories: costs of goods sold (variable costs), operating costs (general and managerial), and capital costs (interest on borrowed money, depreciation, rent). Sales less these costs show a deficit or surplus, if any. The latter is subject to taxation. "Profit" is the net surplus after taxes are paid. From the viewpoint of continuing operations, payments from sales means that resources are reconverted back to cash. As this cash is reinvested in new assets for future sales, to

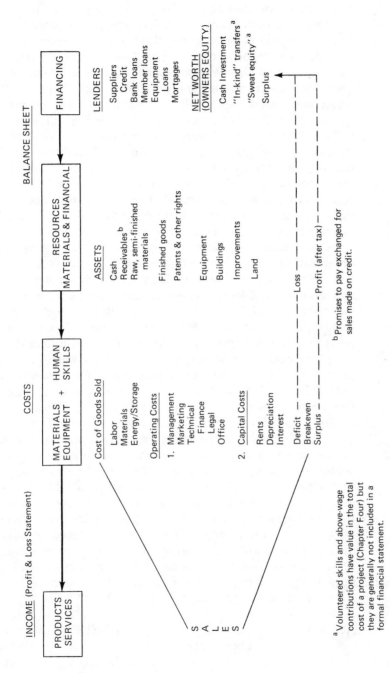

FIGURE 17B. Income, costs, resources, and financing.

repay financial obligations, and to possibly share among owners, different components of the balance sheet are changed.

This cycle of asset acquisition, use, and reconversion to cash includes both short-term "current" assets—those which could be used up in less than a year's time, such as inventory of saleable goods or raw materials—and long-term assets like machinery and office equipment which will be used up over several years. Corresponding changes in the amounts of financing and asset categories reflect shifting use of resources and possibly different types of financing. Short-term liabilities—suppliers' credits or bank financing for changes in inventory or other available resources—and credit for sales are the most common and active. When a building is purchased with credit provided by a long-term loan (mortgage) or if owners are to provide more funds that will be used to buy machinery, significant changes occur in the long-term financing.

The timing of when money comes in and goes out of the organization—when cash sales are made, receivables are collected, and when cash has to be available to pay bills owed such as payroll and suppliers and loan payments—can often be projected from the information that is used to make a balance sheet, and plans for future production and sales. That schedule of payments and receipts is the same type of construction of basic data discussed in Chapter Eight. If reimbursements requests were in fact reliable promises to pay, then you would have a commercial financial cycle. The cash-flow changes are the effects of changes in purchases and sales of assets and financing them. Thus, to accurately design a cash-flow projection for any time period, say 4 months, you would start with the assets you have available (balance sheet) to use, sell, and to finance sales, and plan for what has to be purchased for the sales to be made during the 3 months, and possibly thereafter. Given a level of cash on hand and obligations coming due, you can project ahead what cash will be needed and when to finance the gaps (if any) between the outlay for production and the sales income. Borrowing money is usually based on this type of planning (see Table 8, "Business Cash Budget Projection"). The term "balance sheet" means just that. The costs of assets financed reflects the amounts of and is equal to the financing from different sources, as we see below:

ASSETS	Current	CREDIT	Current
	Long-term		Long-term
		EQUITY	Owners'
		(Net Worth)	contribution
	TOTAL - - - - - - - - = - - - - - - - - TOTAL		

TABLE 8. Business Cash Budget Projection

	December	January	February	March	April	May
		Estimated	4 MONTHS			
Sales	$8,000	$10,000	$12,000	$20,000	$20,000	$10,000
Cash	4,000	5,000	6,000	10,000	10,000	5,000
50% credit for 30 days	8,000	4,000	5,000	6,000	10,000	10,000
Other		—	—	—	—	—
Total Cash Inflow	$12,000	$ 9,000	$11,000	$16,000	$20,000	$15,000
Cost of Productions						
Labor	$ 2,500	$ 3,000	$ 5,000	$ 5,000	$ 2,000	
Materials	5,000	6,000	10,000	10,000	5,000	
General Expenses						
Salaries	$ 1,000	$ 1,000	$ 1,200	$ 1,200	$ 1,200	
General Office	100	100	200	300	200	
Marketing Advertising	1,000	1,000	1,000	1,000	1,000	
Rent	200	200	200	200	200	
Other						
Equipment					2,000	
Taxes	200			2,000		
Total Cash Outflow	$9,800	$11,300	$17,600	$19,700	$11,600	
Surplus (deficit)	$2,300	($2,300)	($6,600)	($3,700)	$ 7,400	
Plus balance at beginning of month	4,000					
Cumulative	$6,200	$ 4,200	($2,400)	($6,100)	$ 2,400	
Financing Needed			$ 3,700	$ 1,300		

The differences between the costs of the resources owned by the organization and what the creditors are owed is the "net worth" of the business.

$$\text{Assets} - \text{Liabilities} = \text{Net Worth}$$

It belongs to the owners and is composed of what they originally put into the business plus surplus generated from sales. The organization has no contractual obligation to distribute it. The owners equity or net worth is the component of the financing at highest risk. Losses are financed by owners, as mentioned earlier, and in the event of bankruptcy or any kind of termination of the business, creditors, including employees who are owed for past work, have prior rights to owners to claim assets to pay off their debts. The owners' capital is at greatest risk, regardless of the nature of the source—cooperative members, state agency development funds, a rich investor, or your aged grandmother's savings.

Certain important considerations should be understood when you make use of financial information:

1. Human productivity is expressed monetarily. The valuation of skills employed in activities are presumed to be fully measured or measurable in the different rates of wages and salaries for different jobs (functions). In a practical way, this type of information is reflected in the employment section of the local newspaper, or from learning what similar organizations are currently paying. Volunteer inputs are not shown in traditional accounting information, even though they might be a significant part of the cost of getting a business started or running it. However, as discussed earlier, they are a true cost of production.

2. Value of the services or goods produced by an enterprise is also measured purely in monetary terms of dollars exchanged in sales.

3. Balance sheets are an historical set of accounts with information that may even include the first day of recorded transactions about the acquisition and use of resources, and their financing. The monetary values are historical, though sometimes adjusted to reflect the current market valuation where not to do so would be seriously misleading. These statements are summaries of different types of transactions, and as such accountants prepare them to "fairly" represent the activities of the organization in financial terms.

DETERMINING DEPRECIATION:
A COST OF PRODUCTION

Insofar as the productivity of an enterprise primarily depends on human skills rather than raw materials, as in sales and marketing organizations, its physical assets necessary for production would most likely be limited to office furniture. Here, as in human services organizations, the major cost component of productivity would be wages. Such resources are paid for as they are employed. But in the financing of a food cooperative, there is often a considerable investment in equipment for operations—e.g., refrigeration, meat-cutting machines, scales, storage racks, cash registers, and so forth. These resources (long-term assets) would make up a significant portion of the total investment in the enterprise. The annual cost associated with their utilization and wearing out in production is called "depreciation." Thus over time, these types of resources are expected to be consumed by the enterprise. They lose their productive value through use. "Useful life" of a given asset is a period of time during which its full cost is expected to be depreciated. For uniformity in accounting practices, the Internal Revenue Service assigns a range of useful life values to many different categories of depreciable assets.

It must be clearly noted that "useful life" is an accounting concept which reflects an attempt to allocate on an annual basis the cost of assets with a productive life of greater than one year. Because it is an accounting concept, not an actual measure of use, an asset may in fact be useable for a much longer time. But the idea is that an annual charge for production is attributable to long-use assets. Thus it can and should be accounted for as a cost component in the selling price. The depreciable value of used assets—i.e., a truck to a new owner—is what they cost the new owner. Depreciation is shown as an annual charge on the income statement. It is also shown as a reduction of value of the asset on the balance sheet under the title of "accumulated" depreciation.

Assume, for example, that the refrigeration equipment in a food cooperative cost $12,000, and its useful life is six years. The annual cost of this equipment component is determined by dividing the useful life into the total cost of the equipment. Thus in each of six years, $2,000 may be "charged" against the value of the equipment and as an annual cost of store operation which is deducted from annual income. Each year the value of the equipment on the balance sheet is reduced by $2,000. The actual calcu-

137

lation of an annual depreciation charge varies depending on the type of accounting method chosen. But depreciation should always be charged into the annual cost of production and accounted for in the pricing so that one-time expenditures for resources may be recovered over their useful lives.

Though depreciation is a "cost" of production, it is not paid out like these other operating expenses. Thus it is referred to as a "non-cash" charge. The full cost of whatever is being depreciated was already paid out at the time of the purchase, either with available cash or with loans or both. Thus the best way to look at and understand what this accounting term is all about is to see that accounting for depreciation is a way to get back the original purchase cost of an asset that will be used over a long period of time. It was paid for in advance of use, therefore an annual charge represents its use and the return of a portion of the cost. If you rented the same piece of equipment, you would have to pay for its periodic use, just as you make rental payments for space. Ownership means that you have purchased a resource and have full right to use it. You can only depreciate what you own. Someone else depreciates what is rented to you. Depreciation is shown as a separate cost or expense category on a profit and loss statement. When you rent, you pay for the right to use a resource for a specific time. Both belong to separate expense categories, but usually refer to resources that are relatively high in cost and are used over a period of time, longer than a year. The balance sheet shows the reduced value of a long-term (capital) asset—the original cost of the resource that you own less the accumulated annual depreciation charges. The undepreciated portion of the asset represents what the business has available for future use—i.e., equipment, furniture, typewriters, vehicles, and the like. Land, though it may change in market value, does not depreciate.

AN OVERVIEW OF BUSINESS FINANCING

Physical resources and human skills often require financing over different periods of time before their use and productivity can be reconverted to cash and be purchased again for continuous production. The cycle of paying out wages and suppliers for materials and financing longer-life assets that are necessary for production is a normal expectation of any business. So too is stocking of inventory and the sale of output on credit. In a food

retailing business, inventory such as popularly consumed items of
fruit juice may have a relatively short "turnover time" from availability on the shelf until it is sold for cash. In terms of the store's
operation, it would probably have a short financing cycle as op-
posed to an item such as expensive canned crabmeat. But initially
the fruit was grown, harvested, processed, shipped, and distributed
before it arrived on the shelf for consideration of the consumer.
Agriculture and processing loans, and distributor sales credit, were
involved for each cycle of economic activity. At each step, the
added value of services and production increased the final price.
People had to be paid for their labor; suppliers had to be paid for
their goods and services. Commercial financing at each level, in
addition to the owners' finance, supported the cash-to-cash cycle
of each entity until the consumers provided the ultimate payment
for all the processes (see Figure 18, "Resource Turnover"). But

FIGURE 18. Resource "turnover."

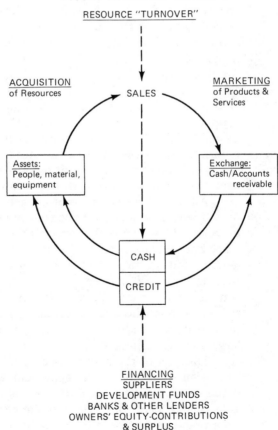

RESOURCE "TURNOVER"

ACQUISITION
of Resources

SALES

MARKETING
of Products &
Services

Assets:
People, material,
equipment

Exchange:
Cash/Accounts
   receivable

CASH

CREDIT

FINANCING
SUPPLIERS
DEVELOPMENT FUNDS
BANKS & OTHER LENDERS
OWNERS' EQUITY-CONTRIBUTIONS
& SURPLUS

fruit juice is purchased, stocked, and resold all the time. The equipment used in refrigeration systems has a much longer cycle of use and productivity. It is necessary for stocking the frozen juices, which are cheaper to buy wholesale than the canned juices. However, its financing cycle is much longer than for storing and selling the juice. Each sale of frozen juice can contribute some small amount to the cost of using this asset each year and over the useable lifetime of the equipment. Either the enterprise paid for this asset initially or it borrowed money to acquire it, using promises to pay rather than cash. Charging for the use is getting it back again for replacement or paying of obligations.

All kinds of commercial financing of short and long term are designed to fit the cycles of productivity and resale of different assets of the enterprise. Banks finance not only the production or purchase of available inventory but also credit sales. Long-term financing is for long-life assets—buildings, trucks, and so forth—the use of which is needed for production but is only a part of the annual cost. So at each economic level, the different enterprises provide time for the buyers to pay the bill for their output. If the supplier or distributor sells the juice on the basis of receiving payment within ten days rather than cash on delivery, then the supplier is financing the inventory of products in the store until the bill is paid. Suppliers themselves are major sources of business credit. Eventually, cash from the sale could be used to pay the supplier's debt if the sale is made within the time that the bill is to be paid. The risk of not selling the item before the bill is due is incurred by the owner(s) of the store. Whether it is a cooperative or an individual or a group of investors, the creditors will only accept a certain level of risk of resale associated with the business.

All creditors expect that owners will have enough of their own financing in an enterprise to share the risk that the assets used up and sold will produce enough to repay the principle of their loans and, when relevant, the interest costs on a timely basis. No lender wants to take the full risk of financing an enterprise—that is, financing 100 percent of the cycle. However, certain public funding sources may provide financing on special terms to high-risk situations where the possible benefits would be increased employment, increased tax revenues, or economic betterment for a large number of people.

The cost of the money used by a borrower is interest charges. The level of interest and repayment terms for the principle are based on the lenders' view of the risk of the enterprise not being able to pay back the loan and the general level of interest rates. As a practical matter, a loan would be for no longer than the useful life of the resource. Thus a loan for seasonal inventory in a clothing store is for three or four months. But if a cash register is purchased, a loan would be for several years. Clearly, as long as depreciation has been charged into the cost of the products being sold, it would be a source of funds from which the principle of a loan could be repaid. Profits from the sales are another source.

You can see that if an enterprise is fairly new, the need for owner's investment is fairly high, because commercial creditors don't know what to expect about either the business idea being successful or the management doing a reasonably competent job of organizing resources and selling output. This is true regardless of whether owners have hopes of making big profits or sharing the benefits of a successful new use of resources with as many users of the products and services as possible. As sales get underway, and more costs are being recovered, more credit is usually available to help finance the production being sold. So your enterprise may go from paying cash on delivery to paying before the next delivery. Then you may have credit of 20 to 30 days from delivery. The point is that long-term financing supplied by owners (equity) needs to be available (1) to initially get the operation started, (2) to support the operating cycle, and (3) to finance, in part or completely, resources whose productivity and utilization (depreciation) cycles extend over a long period of time.

As a business becomes more established, its ability to borrow money to finance resources increases, but lenders always want to see a safety level of owners' capital in case sales fall, the business ideas are not as successful or profitable as everyone expected, or if there are serious management problems. New capital from owners supports expanding business activities and adds to the safety margin that lenders look for on the financing side of the balance sheet. Profits from operations reinvested in the business also represent a source of owners' capital which can help support new loan levels. Thus in general, lenders are concerned with the ratio of the level of debt to the total financing and particularly the level of cash available to make loan payments. But short-term lenders, suppliers, and bankers look at the relationship of current assets—cash, receivables, and saleable inventory—to current debt, including current payments on long-term loans, to determine whether or not there is enough margin to protect their loans.

11

How to Understand
Prices in the Marketplace

PRODUCTION AND MANAGEMENT COSTS

Costs of resources used in production are usually separated into two general categories: (1) Those costs of resources which go directly into making and selling a product or providing a service, and (2) all other resource costs that support the general operations of the enterprise. In the previous chapters, this division has been referred to as direct and indirect costs, or program and administrative support costs. The concept remains the same; however, the terminology generally used for a business operation is "variable" and "fixed" costs. The origin of this perspective is from the accounting of manufacturing costs. Direct costs of labor and materials "vary" proportionately with the volume of production. Each additional unit of production requires additional unit costs of materials and labor; hence the financial view of them as variable costs. Accounting for variable costs does not have to be exclusively limited to the manufacturing viewpoint. Each new McDonalds hamburger operation represents an additional unit of variable cost in relation to the corporation's management costs. Specific revenues can also be related to those costs of the new restaurant unit.

142

Adding a lawyer to a large law firm could even be seen as a variable cost because office rent, equipment, and administrative staff remain essentially the same. The output of any organization can be analyzed in the same manner, regardless of whether the product is hamburgers, education, or counseling services. Each additional unit of production has identifiable costs. These identifiable costs are entitled "costs of goods sold" on an income statement.

Fixed costs are those spent on general operations for administrative functions, capital costs of physical and intangible resources (assets), and financing costs, which are mainly interest on long-term loans. General and administrative costs (G&A) include the personnel and nonpersonnel costs associated with managing the enterprise—salaries, travel, insurance, utilities, advertising, and office supplies. Also included are professional services such as accounting and legal work. All of these costs basically reflect the same type of resources that were required in the management of the Child Abuse Project. There is also the cost to use equipment and space. Rent is for the right to use others' resources. But if the same resources are owned by the business, an annual depreciation cost is calculated. Intangible assets are nonphysical resources associated with exclusive control or ownership such as patents, franchises, distributorships, trade marks, and names. They too are generally used up over time in the same financial way as physical resources. All these resource costs are referred to as "fixed" costs.

Many small-business owners refer to the financial concept of fixed costs as the monthly "nut" or "overhead" they have to meet. Their focus is writing checks each month. Because these costs do not vary appreciably over a range of production and sales volume, they represent the cost of resources that maintain a level of operating capacity. A given space can store or display a limited number of articles for sale. A coordinator or manager is needed from the very earliest days of getting a business started. Activities may grow to a considerable level before an assistant manager is hired. A bookkeeper can change bookkeeping systems to accommodate a growing number of financial transactions. If part of the bookkeeping job is to make a daily bank deposit, the task is required regardless of the amount of the deposit. The resources that are accounted for in the fixed-costs category usually have to be available for ongoing operation, regardless of the level of productive activity. However, some of them, such as advertising, travel, or training, may be "less fixed" than rent or interest charges. On the other hand, when resources such as space and equipment are inefficiently utilized, their full costs still have to be paid. The same is true for how well loan funds are used. Interest costs have to be paid (and repayments too) irrespective of the productive use of resources for which the money was borrowed.

The annual income statement shows these costs on a yearly basis. Thus, the difference between the price that is received for your products or service and the direct (variable) costs to produce it provides a "contribution" per unit or by dollar volume to cover the fixed (managerial and capital) costs. When subtracted from sales revenues, the difference is "gross profits" or profits before charges for administration and capital costs. If the contribution is greater than fixed costs, then a surplus is produced. That surplus is subject to income tax obligations. Here is an example of an annual income statement:

ANNUAL INCOME STATEMENT

I *Sales (Quantity × price per unit)*
_____

   –Variable Costs   (Quantity × variable cost per unit)
   = = = = = = = = = = = = =
   ("Costs of good sold")

II *Contribution Margin*
_____

   (Gross Profit)

   –Fixed Costs
   = = = = = = = = = = = =
   (Managerial and Capital Items)

III *Surplus (deficit)*
_____

   (Pretax Income or Loss)

   –Income Tax
   = = = = = = = = = = = =

IV *Net Income or Loss*
_____

HOW COSTS CHANGE WITH VOLUME OF OUTPUT

Total cost of operating a business combines the direct production or variable costs, which increase (decrease) proportionately with changes in volume, and managerial and capital costs, which remain relatively stable up to a certain level of production (see Figure 19, "Total Cost/Volume of Production").

1. Total cost rises mainly because more additional variable costs are being incurred with increased volume.

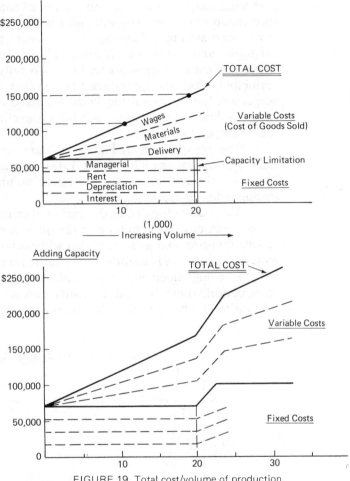

FIGURE 19. Total cost/volume of production.

2. Because fixed costs do not change with volume, each increment of production requires less fixed costs to support it.
3. Because capacity is expanded through additions of equipment and personnel carrying out managerial and technical functions, fixed costs of operations will rise. But higher volume will be possible because of greater capacity.

Now consider the changes in the percentages of the two cost components in each unit of output. As production volume is expanded, unit costs (total costs ÷ number units), whether they are for canned goods or hours of legal services, contain proportionally less and less fixed costs. Because a manager's salary is divided by

145

the total output, that cost component of total cost of each unit of production declines. The total cost per unit falls until the capacity of a given amount of managerial, technical, and physical resources of space and equipment is reached. That level of operation is an ideal volume of business activity which fully utilizes resources. In principle, that level produces the lowest unit cost. Additional capacity, initially resulting in added fixed costs per unit, will, as more volume is generated, produce a declining portion of fixed cost and total unit costs.

The information in Figure 20 shows general, administrative, and capital costs as $70,000 and direct production costs as $4.00 per unit. Table 9 illustrates the effect on unit cost as production is expanded to capacity.

The reason for all this discussion about the intricacies of costs of production is to help look at the question of how to put a price on what you are selling so that you will not lose money. Because resource utilization is calculated in the form of unit costs of whatever is being made and sold, and changes at different levels of production, there is a bit of confusion about how to figure out the prices to be charged. The minimum price for what you pro-

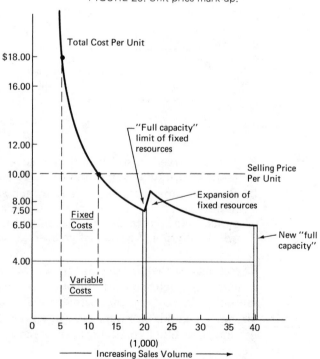

FIGURE 20. Unit price mark-up.

TABLE 9. Cost Change Chart

Number of Units	Fixed Costs	− Variable Costs	= Total Cost	Unit Cost
5,000	$ 70,000	$ 20,000	$ 90,000	$18.00
10,000	70,000	40,000	110,000	11.00
20,000	70,000	80,000	150,000	7.50
25,000	100,000[a]	100,000	200,000	8.00
30,000	100,000	120,000	220,000	7.30
40,000	100,000	160,000	260,000	6.50

[a]Expansion.

duce has to attract buyers as well as cover costs incurred, but at the same time, it is limited by what other businesses are charging for the same or similar products and services. It is limited by competition.

Figure 20, "Unit Price Mark-Up," shows that if a product can be sold at $10.00 there is a minimum level of production and sale which is needed to cover all costs. Fixed costs for a maximum volume of production are the costs for a given period of time. Assume they are for a year. The illustration shows that as volume is increased, the costs of each unit fall steadily. At a selling price of $10.00 per unit, 11,666 units would have to be sold to cover total costs of the sales volume. (Breakeven production level: Number of units = fixed costs ÷ price less variable cost per unit). If you are unable to sell that many units because of a limited market, or if the competitive price is lower, then your project is not economically feasible at that volume. If you could sell 20,000 units, operations would be very profitable since your "mark-up" over variable costs need only be $3.50 per unit to cover all costs of your output. Profit would be $2.50. Thus you could reduce your selling price. At the point where the selling price just equals the cost, $7.50, (assuming a volume of 20,000 units), operations are at "breakeven." Cost of all resources used up in production are recovered: there is neither surplus nor profit. If more capacity is added, unit costs would initially rise and then fall as added fixed costs were divided by more units of production.

The same concept is applicable where you cannot easily count each unit, but only the volume of sales, such as in a variety store or food retailing business. You would determine an average mark-up per wholesale dollar of inventory of goods to be sold that would contribute enough revenues to cover fixed costs. So $50,000 of inventory sold at a 50 percent mark-up ($75,000) would produce $25,000 of gross profits available to pay for general and administrative and capital costs.

147

A RETAIL FOOD COOPERATIVE

To translate these volume/cost calculations into a practical application, consider the example of a retail food cooperative. Categories of fixed costs would include salaries, rent, insurance, depreciation on equipment, interest on borrowed money, utilities and general maintenance, legal, accounting, and advertising services. While these may vary somewhat from month to month, they are all necessary costs for this type of business during a year of operations. Variable costs would include the wholesale price of food and other items sold ("cost of goods sold"), plus a couple of percentage points to represent normal spoilage and "shrinkage," loss from damage and theft. Thinking in terms of dollar volume, you would calculate a percentage of mark-up over a level of annual variable costs that would have to be charged in order to pay all the fixed costs, and still be competitive. Table 10, "Monthly Financial Report—A Cooperative Food Store," shows actual operating costs of a large store for two succeeding months. Sales vary because of a normal seasonal fluctuation. The percentage mark-up from the wholesale costs of goods sold is stable, but the March sales level is below the point where the contribution margin—gross profits— covers all the fixed costs. In the following month more than enough sales to cover these costs occurred, thus there was a surplus. So the average monthly sales volume needed to operate at "breakeven" level is around $112,000. Sales volume for the year must produce enough gross profits to cover twelve times the average monthly fixed costs (monthly "nut") of about $13,700. If the operating expenses are reduced—less advertising, more volunteer work, reduced committee expenses—then the minimum volume of sales needed to cover all costs would be lower than $112,000 per month. If prices could be raised so that the gross profit margin were greater, sales volume could also be at a lower level. The gross profit figures for each month (or any period of time) are derived from tallying the cash-register receipts and subtracting the cost of goods sold. That is the difference between the "opening inventory," or goods available for sale, at the beginning of March plus purchases, less the "closing" inventory, that which is left at the end of the month. The value of goods unsold at the end of the month is in fact the "opening" inventory of the next month. For any ongoing business, inventory should be counted periodically, otherwise there is no way of knowing the cost of the sales or how to determine what is available for future sales. The

TABLE 10. Monthly Financial Report—A Cooperative Food Store.

	April 1980	%	March 1980	%
TOTAL SALES	$113,334	114.6	$97,410	114.6
Cost of Goods Sold				
Variable Cost	98,915	100.0	85,000	100.0
Gross Profit ("Mark-Up")	$ 14,419	14.6	$12,410	14.6
Operating Expenses				
Payroll	$ 7,450		$ 7,531	
Rent	1,000		1,000	
Utilities	1,501		1,377	
Telephone	130		100	
Insurance	941		606	
Advertising	122		30	
Interest	42		45	
Depreciation	632		632	
Maintenance	158		89	
Market area	1,298		1,579	
Spoilage—unusual	12		—	
Office supplies	41		162	
Committees	345		305	
Theft/bad checks	—		—	
Bank charges	120		125	
Miscellaneous	50		50	
TOTAL	$ 13,842		$13,636	
NET INCOME (LOSS)	$ 577		($1,226)	

other cost figures in this illustration are from the actual monthly expense records with the exception of "depreciation," an annual non-cash charge attributed to the "using up" of expensive long-lasting (capital) resources such as refrigeration equipment, scales, storage racks, and so forth.

Private profit-making organizations search for the best use of budgeted dollars in terms of improving the productive relationship between fixed and variable cost resources. In a business setting, if wages and administrative salaries are to increase, volume has to be expanded, prices increased, or productivity improved (increased contribution margin per unit of sales). Generating new volume may also mean that new investment in facilities and expanded stock of inventory has to take place. Sometimes nonprofit attitudes obscure the universality of the issue of productive use of managerial resources.

149

Costs of nonprofit service organizations are paid by funding sources who are not user/consumers. There is no market pricing mechanism for their output that influences efficient use of administrative and capital resources. However, minimizing the unit cost to produce a service by spreading the management support costs over all the programs is still a valid focus for assessing effective utilization of resources.

Managers of a business enterprise can often obtain industry financial statistics which provide typical cost ratios and financial standards for their type of business operations—i.e., gross profit margins, advertising costs to sales, salaries to sales, sales volume to space, and so forth. Many banks and other lenders compare industry averages with the components of a company's financial reports in order to help make judgments about financial capacity of an enterprise to use borrowed funds and the managerial capability as measured by efficient resource use. This statistical information is often available from trade associations and from commercial credit rating agencies (see Appendix D). These statistics provide general guidelines of industry ratios. They are averages derived from a large number of enterprises. Given an individual enterprise, variances in cost components can represent the high productivity of different resource elements or poor management. For example, operating costs of a self-service mini-market may not easily be compared with a family-owned food store that provides customer services, even though they both have the same dollar volume of business. The first may stress much more advertising, the second, more employee costs as a portion of sales. If a profit-making food retailer were to be compared with a cooperative doing the same volume of sales, considerable adjustment to total cost would have to be made for the value of volunteer labor inputs. Once again you can see that volunteer input has a commercial value when related to the costs of skills required by a business. Industry statistics on food retailing can provide valuable comparisons about competitive mark-up, space costs as a percentage of volume, advertising, "shrinkage," and other significant relationships of both variable fixed costs and volume of sales.

Regardless of the availability of this type of cost information, the competitive price and resource cost factors of a particular market or industry should be investigated by those trying to develop a new business. In order to have an economically viable enterprise, total costs of operations have to be covered within a competitive environment.

VOLUNTEERS:
COSTS, BENEFITS, AND EFFICIENCY

As noted earlier, volunteer and "in-kind" contributions are not accounted for in financial reporting documents and are often left out of calculations of project costs. When costs of organizationally essential skills from volunteers are not charged in some way to the price calculation, budget estimates are based only on cash needs. The overall planning of not-for-profit businesses often assumes the availability of valuable contributed resources, and usually does not adequately "account" for them. Consequently, the "cost" of the goods and services produced and sold is less than what the competitive marketplace would show for ventures of equivalent risk. What is really happening?

1. Risk to the financial sources is being reduced because less money is required from them to get an enterprise going. Those who are providing resources on a "free" or non-market basis are absorbing part of the risk.
2. The level of sales where financial cost is covered by operating revenues is reduced if many resources of a fixed and variable cost nature, primarily wages and salaried activity, are volunteered or equipment donated. Therefore a reduced volume of revenues is necessary only to cover the financial outlay for purchased resources.
3. Volunteers are subsidizing the enterprise. Owners/members of a cooperative who pay in capital, and lenders, share the financial risk of sales volume which does not pay for resources used. Those who also volunteer their labor subsidize the financial risk by reducing the level of paid resources.

Effective management of resources by a cooperative enterprise can contribute to lower costs and thus provide greater benefits to users. But the organizational risk involved in assuring productive use of volunteer resources is considerable. Generally, costs are saved because of substituted "free" labor of volunteers. But functions left to volunteer efforts may not be performed adequately or on a timely basis, thus creating inefficient organization and wasted resources. It may be better to pay someone to organize various management functions of operating a business rather than to rely on volunteer labor. In that way, an explicit contract of accountability for performing specific and critical functions can be set up

151

for the organization. Though a few pennies may be added to the final cost of the output, they may warrant significant savings in managing other resources.

THE "BREAKEVEN LEVEL" OF SALES

With an understanding of the meaning and relationship of variable and fixed costs, organizers and managers can make elementary estimates of the costs of operations at different levels of production or volume of sales. Consequently, they can determine the relationship of prices per unit that have to be charged and overall revenues to estimated costs and volumes.

The breakeven level, the operating level at which total costs equal revenues, is the objective toward which the work of business planning and financial projections of costs and revenues is oriented. Arriving at the total costs estimate for that level requires a good deal of practical thinking about the management functions that will be done to start and build a dependable sales volume. Each kind of business has a different emphasis on the managerial functions, and the financial and physical resources. The operations of a credit union involve considerable spending on activities that generate membership savings, loan processing, and collections. Retail businesses are cash-oriented, with heavy emphasis on advertising, customer relations, and maintaining saleable stock. Manufacturing has a totally different management direction toward work processing and investment in equipment, raw materials, and labor, and sometimes considerable effort of managing credit sales. Since sales are an essential focus of any business enterprise, marketing functions to be performed and their required resources have to be carefully analyzed and accounted for in cost estimates. There are no formulas for marketing expenditures for a particular enterprise. While there may be plenty of marketing information, every business uses it in its own special way. New businesses often rely on new ways to promote and sell their services and products in their efforts to create customer response.

MARKETING EMPHASIS

The business plan for a new enterprise basically consists of answering the question of how you get from your idea to a level of operation that is financially self-supporting. While obtaining full financial support is an objective of other nonprofit activities, there is a basic difference. The marketing function to reach the consumer/user is considerably more complex than the marketing to funding sources (grant providers, etc.) who are not users of the products or services of the organization they finance. The consumer public is the ultimate financial test for your efforts of promoting a business enterprise, and that is true regardless of whether profits are a part of organizational objectives or not. Because an enterprise is not for profit does not mean that it will automatically fulfill needs of the consumer/users, or cause them to easily part with their money. Organizing a not-for-profit cooperative form of enterprise does not eliminate the need to clearly determine the purpose and strategy for carrying out the activities of the enterprise, including the conscious effort to find and maintain a "market" for the output. The costs of marketing—all the tasks associated with presenting, reaching, and selling products and services—reflect a search to find who will *pay* for what you think needs to be produced as well as who wants it. The "who" and "what price" questions compose a dynamic framework. Thus marketing may have a high element of experimentation costs because the introduction of new ideas and products is an innovative activity in a constantly shifting environment of consumer needs, expectations and ability to pay.

The marketing orientation of a business plan has to respond to defining and meeting the changing interests and trends of the consumer/user and develop a strategy to meet competition, actual or potential. A clear understanding of why current product availability and market structure do *not* "satisfy" consumers—price, availability, fulfillment of needs, repair services, and the like—is the starting point for a marketing plan, as well as for determining the types of products or services that will be attractive and saleable.

In planning and operating an enterprise, considerable attention has to be directed toward developing and even creating an effective demand from the consumer/user for the output of the project. While there are some situations in which consumer alternatives (choices) may be limited and a noncompetitive environment for new commercial activities seems obvious, such situations are rare. There are never any guarantees that the economic and other conditions which initially fostered feasibility and success of an enterprise will continue to positively influence sales and volume of business. Marketing is an ongoing function. It is continuous evaluation of sales trends and selling opportunities. The results become a guide to owners and managers about the direction for decisions regarding future investment in and uses of resources. Consumer/users have to be continually attracted to and find value in their purchases from an enterprise. But beware—new economic activities and uses of resources stimulate other responses to new market conditions and consumer/user preferences. Planners, organizers, managers, and investors can always expect others to copy their ideas if they are successful. Such competition has a surprising way of requiring investors and managers to be on their toes to improve and change their products and services in response to market conditions. While this highlighting of marketing functions may seem obvious to many readers, it is too often not made an express part of organizing small-business activities. So operations and activities planning are incomplete without explicitly defining and redefining the functions presumed to be necessary to make the final sale of the output of the organization. Translation of the costs of the functions is guided by the same managerial and financial principles discussed in the planning chapters of this book.

In summary, marketing functions are often a critical element of operating costs, since sales volume may be highly influenced by their presence or absence. A marketing plan that answers the questions of how you will sell products or services and to whom is a must for any enterprise.

OTHER PLANNING CONSIDERATIONS

Depending on the business, consideration must be given to location, availability of transportation, and availability of skills necessary for the particular operations. Availability of resources such as supplies and raw materials may be essential, especially in processing enterprises. "Availability" depends on the number of supply sources and conditions. It may translate into higher than assumed costs, when alternative sources and activities have to be planned for. Legal and accounting services have a greater emphasis in business operations because the commercial relations with suppliers of financial and other resources and consumers are more clearly defined on a contract basis. While the need is of the same relevance in non–business organizations, there is usually less awareness about these functions.

Getting Assistance

Learning the significance of business terms and concepts and gaining an understanding of financial management of resources in an enterprise may take time and help. The U.S. Small Business Administration (SBA) can be particularly useful as a source of readable and practical publications on many subjects pertaining to small-business planning, finance, and managerial activities. It also has "profiles" of different businesses and discussions of problems by industry grouping. Many of their publications are free and those that are not are very reasonably priced. Appendixes B and C are lists, respectively, of SBA Field Offices and some of the useful publications available. SCORE is a subdivision of the SBA. It stands for Service Corps of Retired Executives who are available for volunteer consulting work through the SBA. While most of these people do not have a background in the nonprofit sector, they often have technical and general managerial business experience that may be useful to help formulate your plans and improve operations.

Some universities also sponsor small-business development centers where various kinds of assistance may be available. The National Consumers Cooperatives Bank, through its regional offices, is also building the capability of assisting cooperative activities that include housing, production, and consumer operations.

V

GOVERNANCE

12

Governance and
Financial Management

PURPOSE AND FUNCTIONING OF
GOVERNING BOARDS

The role of the board of directors, trustees, or any other governing body of a nonprofit organization is not unlike that of a board of a private profit-making organization. The job of the latter is to tend to the well-being of the corporation in the greatest long-term interest of the stockholders. In a similar sense, those who act for the "stockholders" of a private non-profit organization have a dual role: 1) they are representatives of the public beneficiaries whose interests the organization serves, and 2) they are the policy-making body and financial controllers of a legal and economic entity. They oversee investment and operations for the purpose of maximizing social and economic benefit produced through the medium of their organization. Part of the transition from using personally controlled resources for one's own choices to organizing and using publicly available resources for the public interest is the empowering of a governing body to interpret and guide the organization in achieving its goals. ("Public" here is understood to mean other people's money, government and private, *and* the needs of the

159

group served. The needs may be of a broad order—e.g., those of the mentally retarded of the nation—or of a small interest group such as a local softball club.) Hence a governing body's roles are representative of somewhat diverse views regarding a public good and a "trustee" for resources under control of an organization and the decisions to use them in a certain way. *How* the governing functions are constituted—through trustees, a collective of workers, total membership, a steering committee, and so forth—should not be confused with the nature of the work that has to be done, nor the high level of responsibility the participants have.

According to traditional charity wisdom, boards of trustees exercise a stewardship role, one which seems to blend (and confuse) public volunteerism as a duty of the religiously enlightened, with charitable causes involving the less enlightened or "less fortunate." The premise of this book, however, is that "doing good" is not enough. More precisely and positively stated, "doing good is managing well." And managing well has to do with clarity of purpose and using resources innovatively, efficiently, and responsibly. Most businesspeople who are on boards of private corporations have just this same concern. While making a profit is an important orientation of a private business, that consideration does not obscure the more universal and underlying functions of all governance bodies.

In its simplest description, the overriding role of the governing body is to attend on a regular basis to the question of "What is our purpose?" As noted earlier, to reach out for public funds usually also entails legal requirements of selecting corporate officers and creating a governance body to act as "trustees" over resources and as interpreters for the pursuit of the organization's goals. These formal requirements are intended to establish public accountability of the entity for its use of other people's funds. Thus the officers and the board are ultimately liable for the misuse and misappropriation of funds and resources of the organization.

From the view of the financial accountability role of the governance body and all the financial management tasks that should be done by the operating staff, it is clear that a manager has a lonely and difficult job of running an organization without assistance in dealing with many of the financial management responsibilities and issues described in earlier chapters. If the governance body of an organization is without someone or several people who can explain both business and financial problems to other governance participants, as well as assist operating personnel, then there is a critically serious gap in the financial management function of the organization. Furthermore, a governance body itself cannot fulfill its responsibilities to funding sources, nor can it effectively plan and review operations, without significant input of financial skills. In a legal sense, financial management cannot be left solely to the manager, since accountability for use of resources ultimately remains with the governance body and specifically with the officers of the organization. As a practical matter, there are always financial implications to a manager's decisions which need to be shared, explored, and often given direction.

The governance body responds to or should be responsive to those who invest in the organization's purpose and potential to fill a need. This mediating and interpreting role between investor and organizational definition are ever-present, and always implied by each act of the organization. Every purchase made, every project undertaken, every fund drive, every representation of how money is and will be used in an organization, directly relates to the purpose of its existence. The governing body is responsible for asking the questions about interpretation of purpose and how it is reflected in priorities of specific activities. Its job is to develop policy and operating philosophy which interprets the purpose both within and for the organization definition to the public. It is ultimately accountable for the consequences of decisions made by the organization staff, as shown in the following table.

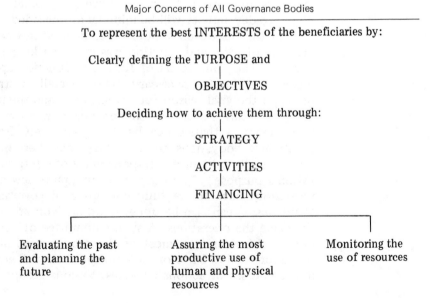

Major Concerns of All Governance Bodies

To represent the best INTERESTS of the beneficiaries by:

Clearly defining the PURPOSE and

OBJECTIVES

Deciding how to achieve them through:

STRATEGY

ACTIVITIES

FINANCING

| Evaluating the past and planning the future | Assuring the most productive use of human and physical resources | Monitoring the use of resources |

CHARACTER AND COMPOSITION

Governing boards, like programs, should mirror the organizational functions that are key to their success at any given time. For example, a program that is just starting usually needs a majority of governing members who may be able to assist in organizing functions—seeing to public relations and liaison; raising money; making business decisions about office space and other major business commitments; providing legal assistance for tax exemption, by-laws, and contractual arrangements; and setting up financial records if necessary. The governing board of a more established organization is (or should be) involved in evaluating the effects of its programs, clarifying its operational objectives and future direction, and making sure it best represents the public interest and that its managers are using resources as efficiently as possible. Governance tasks reflect a different "state" of organizational development, which requires an emphasis on skills of evaluation and planning, rather than marketing and start-up organizing. In order to be fruitful, the resources of the governing board itself must change to fulfill the operational changes from start-up to maturity. Thus, to form a board of directors or a governing committee of any sort whose membership possesses a narrow range of skills and experience is to invite, in the not-too-distant future, organizational crisis and possibly collapse. The ability of such membership to support administrative and programmatic managers of day-to-day activity will be minimal or one-sided.

In the discussion about "organization" in Chapter Two, the problem of form and function was explored in the organizational context. The same focus of form and function applies to governance questions. It is necessary that the overall governance activities focus on the vital reason for its existence and the particular operating structure needed as the organization grows and changes. Since many activities can be done separately from an official governance body, it is not necessary that there be a huge group who formally take on the responsibility of interpreting the organization's purpose. For example, a program-review group does not necessarily have to be fully composed of governance members. Fund raising can also be done by others who are concerned with financing the operations. A small committee of governance members might attend to most of the problems of normal business operations and defer to or recommend to the full governance body major courses of actions or issues. Various groups or committees composed of clients/consumers, staff, and board members, and even public officials might tie in with the governance activities of an organization. All depends on the particular relationships with the public they serve, and the type of activities of the organization. Since these may be changing elements, the priorities of governance and guidance often shift.

While there may be reporting and licensing (legal) requirements for unincorporated as well as incorporated organizations, there is no fixed approach or format for the way decisions have to be made in either. Officers may be empowered with considerable authority or little at all to make decisions for or represent an organization. Decision making can be a joint effort of employees, volunteers, and public representatives—a hierarchical effort or a revolving one. Individuals can be empowered for specific short-lived purposes or regular ongoing functions. People with special or technical capabilities such as consultants are resources to be employed when functionally necessary both at the operating and at the governance levels. Functionally they may fill an ongoing need or only an occasional one.

Some guiding elements about governance participants and organizational environment are worth noting:

DIVERSITY OF PARTICIPATION.
1. Whenever possible, different personal and professional skills and orientation should be available for both governance deliberations and support of the management of activities. Organizing and operating activities is a multidimensional and evershifting effort. While everyone may have the same purpose, a diversity of skills is needed to be successful, to make an impact. (That diversity is suggested in Chapter Two in the section entitled "Overview of Skills Requirements.") However, people with diverse views and talents have to start with a clear agreement of what they are mutually trying to do. Without an explicit agreement, the experience of translating the organization's purpose(s) into operating results can easily become bitter and confusing, rather than stimulating and productive. Because certain technical skills are always essential to any organizational effort, no governance body is complete without financially oriented person(s) and a legal advisor or easy access to one.

FLUIDITY IN THE CHANGE OF PARTICIPANTS
2. New views and energy can only come from new faces. People who are in the same position or environment for too long

often lose their ability to probe and find solutions to new problems. They tend also to prevent others from trying to look at old problems or traditional methods in new ways. ("Oh, we tried that before," or "You have some good ideas there, but...") The organization of change requires new views of new people, even at the risk of repeating things that have been done in the past. On the other hand, a certain amount of continuity is essential to productive decision making. For example, it may be much more effective to "stagger" board membership than to form a whole new board every two years or so. Thus a board of twelve would have six new faces every year. If you have three-year elections or appointments, four persons would be new each year. The position of chairperson could rotate, not only for purposes of "equal power" but for the experience of different styles and expression.

EMPHASIS ON INTERRELATIONSHIP OF DECISION MAKING.
3. Decision making occurs in all activities in an organization. It is the action of people at all levels carrying out their particular tasks within the organizational plans. The financial management functions, for example, run throughout the organization, and each part is dependent on the other—budgeting, cash-flow planning, purchasing, bookkeeping, and reporting. Organization of the flow of financial decisions derives from an understanding of the interrelationships of these functions, rather than of whose job is more important. Thus, structure of management controls should be derived from the translation of purpose(s). They set operating limitations for each type of decision rather than preset ideas about how an organization "should" be.

THE FLOW OF INFORMATION.
4. This is dependent on all the preceding elements. Information about the outcome of an organization's activities or lack thereof is critical to operating and managing responsively. Information, whether favorable or unfavorable, is essential to assessment of what has been done and what you plan to do. Being "surprised," dealing with the "somebody told me," strikes, and facing sudden "demands" by workers or consumers only means that people in the organization and outside it are not being heard or given a chance to communicate their experience to those responsible for its management, self-evaluation, and goal interpretation. Those situations are clear indicators that the full scope of operations and reporting are neither being encouraged nor being carried out.

Governance members should be selected for a reason, and be self-selecting. It is not necessarily enough to want to do something for a cause, or represent a particular group, or help a friend. Since a governing board has overall programmatic and financial accountability for all activities, each member can have a specific role or follow his or her interest—public relations, financial and business operations, personnel policy, legal matters, program planning, policy issues. It is surprising how many small nonprofit organizations choose their board members because of their involvement in "the cause" or assumed "political" connections, rather than by the skills and special experience they might bring to a governing body and to an organization's personnel. Businesspeople, if invited onto a board, are generally there because they are perceived as a source of money, rather than as a potential resource for dealing with issues of management and business operations. Unfortunately, it is a common occurrence that administrative functions of finance and business operation are completely unrepresented by persons in a governing body, even though they are essential to all organizations. Since governance members are advisors to one another insofar as they represent different skills and experience, the lack of representation of business and financial or other important skills means that members are without their own critical assistance when considering direction, new financing arrangements, and managerial issues.

Why are you a board member or why do you want to be one? Where are your best talents most productively applied to the operation of an organization? These are questions to ask yourself (and others) when considering actual or intended participation in an organization. They are also the same questions staff and managers should use to assess the board's capabilities to meet their needs. Thus, to have the governance board of a day-care center totally composed of the parents of children in the program usually creates serious organization problems. Certainly the interests of consumer representation will be filled, but how will other organizational functions be fulfilled? Unless these individuals provide other management skills and experience handling organization problems, *and* their peers appreciate the different basic skills needed by members of the governing body, managerial accountability will be in severe jeopardy. The planning of governance participation requires the

165

efforts of translating the applicability of its members' skills into activities and functions, just as is true of planning for any other activities.

COMMON FINANCIAL MISMANAGEMENT: TWO BASIC EXAMPLES

There are situations in which governance members literally turn over all matters of financial management to a volunteer treasurer whose work and participation become unquestioned, even though it may be undermining the progress of the organization. In this situation, the mystique of finance is perpetuated by governance participants to the detriment of the managers, who often find that the tasks of payment of bills, deposit of receipts, and preparing financial information is totally out of their hands. Their own financial status reviews cannot take place; they are without knowledge of the current financial situation because the checkbook is exclusively under the control of the treasurer. Either few financial reports are made to other members of the governance committee or some type of accounting report is presented without explanation or even relevance to planning and program operations. Other governance members are intimidated, because they are not "experts." There is no way for them to understand or evaluate the "contribution" of the volunteer treasurer. The treasurer becomes the absolute authority, even though everyday planning and spending decisions have to be carried out by the manager. While this may appear to some people to be "good control" over the finances, there is in fact no control at all on the part of the governance body as a whole. Yet the group is still responsible for the organization. Furthermore, this type of control undermines decision-making throughout the organization, creating an unnecessary hierarchical emphasis for implementing the board's part of the program and financial accountability of the organization at the operating level. The board members cannot delegate financial decision-making responsibilities of the simplest order.

Another extreme situation is one in which the manager or executive director makes all the financial decisions. There may be a formal budget or only a very general one that is changed arbitrarily or when crises arise. Board members are assured that everything is going well when they ask. Most of the time they don't ask. The treasurer, if there is one, does not know what his or her function is. While original budgets may be presented for approval, there is no follow-up reporting to see what has happened to the funds. While there is not necessarily a devious intent on the part of the manager, there is a situation of no accountability to the board of governance, and board members do not require it of their employees. The operating budget is in effect a secret.

A variation of this theme occurs when the executive director or coordinator is "not a financial person" and all such matters are handled by the secretary, business manager, or bookkeeper. Since this employee works for the executive director, the latter has full access to any funds he or she thinks are necessary. Everyone else's requests or decisions go through or are subject to the review and authorization of the employee. While there may be adequate documentation of all the transactions, there are the problems of lack of interest on the part of the manager and problems → relating to final control and review by the board of governance. This can be a fairly innocent situation where funds are not misused, only mismanaged. Moneys are spent without relationship to organization rationale. One person makes an arbitrary decision.

AN EXECUTIVE COMMITTEE: MANAGING THE MANAGER

An "executive committee" is usually found on the boards of directors of large private profit-making and nonprofit organizations. This body comprises an advisory group which works with top management to review and advise on major organizational issues. Members meet more frequently than the full board and act as a backup to the management. But because they represent the longer-term interest of the organization, they have a separable and often wider perspective than the manager. They are in effect the link between the overall governance role and the managers' decision making regarding policy interpretation at the highest operating level of the organization. This link is a functional one that is necessary regardless of the size of an organization. After all, a board only meets every month or two and sees the results of managers' decisions after they are made (review) or helps develop the guidelines for future decisions (planning). The executive committee represents ongoing board-level participation to assist in the implementation of policy and plans. Thus, for a board to be most productive in its work of governance, in most instances, it will need to have the equivalent of an executive committee. The number of persons in this function can vary with the organization's size, but the type of person involved must be able to offer timely and useful managerial experience.

In the context of the flow of decisions in an organization, people who carry out this function have a dual role. They provide administrative support to the manager, and can act as interpreters to and for other board members. The two extreme situations cited in the preceding examples could be greatly reduced or eliminated through the operation of some type of executive committee. The manager usually has to be guided or managed by the board, since he or she is in fact an employee of the organization. If there are gaps in the manager's diverse responsibilities or the chain of board accountability to the organization, they have to be seen and responded to. The manager, on the other hand, needs "explainers" on the board, and the availability of practical advice. Without people who possess skills to understand and satisfy these critical

FIGURE 21. Decision spheres.

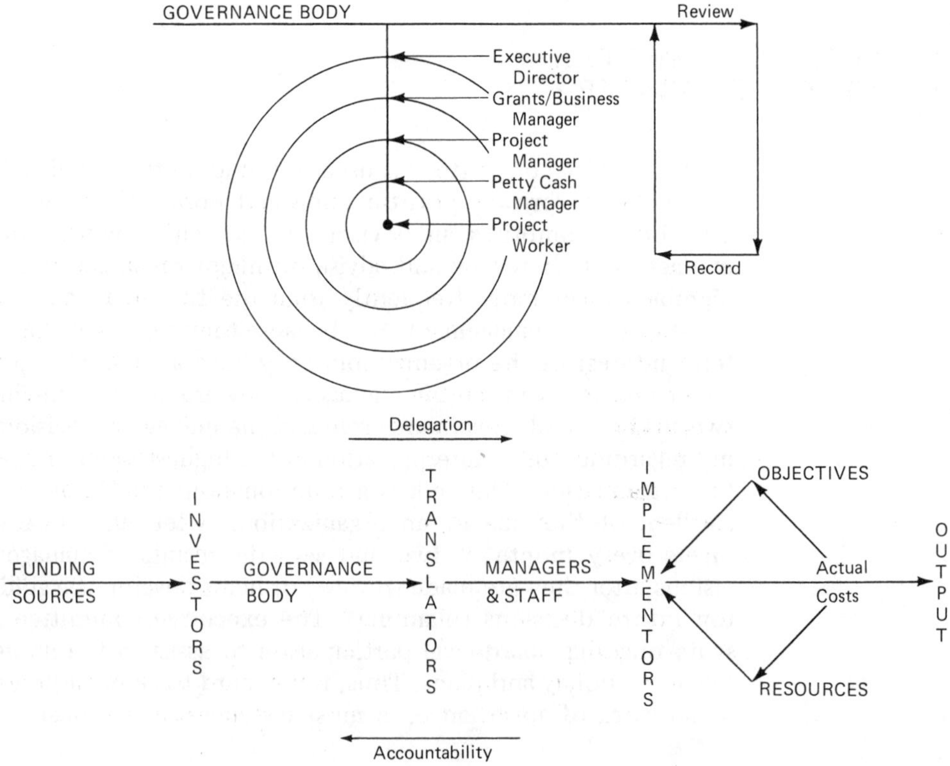

translation and communication needs, a governance board cannot function and the manager's productivity is limited.

THE INTERRELATIONSHIP OF DECISIONS

Rather than think of organizational decision making in terms of hierarchical control, it is more fruitful to perceive it in terms of effects on other decision makers at different points of program implementation. Almost everyone is involved in some type of financial decision making regarding program or managerial activities (See Figure 21 "Decision Spheres"). The decisions of the governance board guide the operating decisions as well as respond to the "investors'" purpose. In a financial management sense, budgetary decisions by the governance board are a matter of direction and allocation of limited resources. The manager's role is to authorize and delegate daily spending decisions based on those criteria. When the original budget projections prove to be unworkable in relation to actual implementation costs and revenue flows, then they must be jointly revised by both managers and governance board. Because the original projections were based on joint expectations, the revisions are, too.

The chain of delegation and accountability starts at a point where financial decisions have the greatest effect on the actions of others (governance board funding sources), and it ends in the decision to purchase a 79¢ item with petty cash. Delegation of spending authority becomes the basis for productively organizing the purchasing activity of the organization. It signifies teamwork because of the interdependency of the roles of the governance board and the implementers. It means that at each level, decision making is guided by a central plan. But it does not mean that the board member makes the decision about a need to buy the 79¢ item or even the $200 typewriter. That can only be made by the persons who see that the item may be necessary in carrying out specific tasks. The governance activities are to look at the larger meaning and budgetary direction of the organization. As a matter of direct accountability, a governance body may reserve for itself certain major spending approvals—i.e., hiring senior staff and consultants—or make spending limits at the different levels of decision making—i.e., petty cash or major expenditures. While choices are made at each level of implementation, they are ultimately subject to governance review and the questions of whether and how expenditures are serving the purpose of the organization.

Authorization and delegation derive from answers to those questions in the form of financial allocation and only incidentally from who is in charge. It is when purpose is not defined in program planning and budgeting that authorization becomes hierarchical authority and accountability becomes arbitrary.

SUCCESS MEANS MORE PLANNING

Resource availability changes constantly; investors need to change their own objectives and directions as economic and social conditions change. What has happened to the objectives of family service organizations during the past twenty years of sharply rising divorce rates and two-income families? What direction has the Boy Scouts of America taken as Suburbia has become a way of middle-class American life and camping a common family activity? The makers of bowling equipment and the Department of Mental Health are strange bedfellows. They have been subject to the same problem of interpreting investment objectives and resource allocation priorities as they have watched and tried to measure these shifts in American family life.

It does not follow that because there is a structure of delegation and accountability, a program or an investment direction will be successful. All the best people working together cannot guarantee that the purpose of an organization is permanent, nor that their interpretation of what should be done, both at the policy level and the operating level, necessarily will be "right." There is always the hindsight that resources should have been directed in some other way, or that if you had only waited a while, conditions would have been different. Nonsense! In profit-making or non-profit organizations, people generally try to use their best judgments concerning what is needed and what is the best use of resources available. Always part of any undertaking is the risk that the purpose of an organization as expressed in its objectives may not prove to be as vital and useful as the perceptions of both managers and governance participants see them. The nonprofit sector is competitive, not only in seeking funding, but in the realm of innovation. Different people and organizations try to figure out how to resolve both the organizational and programmatic responses to unmet needs by using resources according to their particular visions. Thus, programs and organizations die of natural causes—obsolescence and competition—as well as from mismanagement, lack of elementary planning, and control.

The potential of new projects and funding sources invariably opens different programs and investment funding channels. They induce assessment of availability of organizational resources, as we have already seen. Successful achievement of funding for a project is cause for celebration. But in organizational terms, it is also a signal to reconsider what the organization has been doing and will do to further define and achieve its purpose(s). Thus, expanding and moving ahead in actualizing the organizational purpose(s) creates a constant opportunity to ask, "What should we do next?" New programs and directions always create new sets of organizing problems and rearrangement of management functions that require a redefinition of priorities of how resources will be used. A common experience of many rapid-growth organizations is that they outgrow their bookkeeping systems and lose control of the financial information. Ongoing evaluation and planning will help an organization avoid this problem.

In the ongoing organizational context, success is illusive because funding sources and directions constantly shift to new programs and explorations of changing needs. In the early 1970s there was considerable money available for drug-addiction intervention and treatment for the youth of the nation. Those funds have declined over the past few years. The use of drugs has also shifted among population groups. Alcohol abuse has "come back" among the youthful population, and there is more funding for that substance abuse relative to the past years. The awareness of the incidence of drinking among young and middle-aged women has increased considerably such that it is rapidly approaching the same level held by men. Licit drug addiction (tranquilizers) too has been recognized as a drug problem within the last five years. Funding response to abuse of the combination of drugs and alcohol for middle-class Americans is a relatively new direction in mental health. While the various abuse phenomena have been known for years, shifts in funding have been gradual and subject to bureaucratic politics, legislative priorities, and media events.

If your organization had started with funds for drug-addiction services for youth six years ago, where would it be now? Most likely out of business, unless its managers and particularly its governing board said to itself: (1) These monies will not go on forever, even though the problem we are dealing with is enormous and of high national and local priority; (2) What else can we do about this problem and population that makes sense for us (fits our goals), given our resources and the way we can or will operate? It is not up to the board alone to answer this question. But it is the role of the boardmembers to ask it and to help provide for the continuous answering of the question. The question should be asked regularly, at the least at the time of the annual review of the budget and the activities it represents. But it is a special consideration each time the officers or representatives are about to sign an agreement that provides new funds or sets forth a proposal seeking new funding. In the answers to the questions What are your services today? and To whom are they going?, the seeds of tomorrow's planning are being planted.

A major and ongoing function of the governance is program (or investment) planning and review. Yesterday and today are easily defended by managers, staff, and governance participants whose focus is on day-to-day activities. The justification for entering into many new activities and agreements is sometimes based on reasons that have little to do with conscious choice and direction. "This contract will last for years." "There is some easy money for us to get if we go in that direction." "Such and such agency wants us to handle this contract." "We'll go after that one because we can make some money and support the activities we really want to do." "We can get the rest of the money by the end of the year." Too often an organization pursues funding simply because it is there, rather than as a consequence of careful planning of determining where it wants to go in terms of a program of financial objectives. Looking for funding is, in fact, made easier by careful work in financial planning. The hard answers from which policy is developed and plans for activities are made do not come from expedient decisions to undertake new projects and yesterday's formulas for successful operations and funding. That is how board decisions become automatic and nonfunctional, and managers become Lone Rangers with silver bullets.

THE FINANCIAL MANAGEMENT JOB OF THE GOVERNANCE BODY

The many dimensions of the meaning of "review" for the board of governance of any organization, as well as the managers, fall into two categories: program activities and organization management. Since financial planning and reviews reflect the use of resources by an organization, it is not something only the financial specialists do. It is the job of the governance body as a whole to review both the results of individual programs and projects *and* the organizational direction. The treasurer's role is one of organizing and overseeing financial information and reporting (page 17) and possibly assisting in the overall translation of program plans into financial planning. However, one of the most important tasks of the treasurer in his or her relationship with other board activities is to make sure that the financial reporting is informative, understandable and timely.

Since a budget is a financial plan of work that the organization intends to carry out, it is an important responsibility of the chief administrator and financial manager to organize the preparation of annual work plans and budgets for discussion, review, and approval by the governance body. Even in very small organizations, staff and board should set time aside to look at what they have done, and agree to what they would like to achieve before each fiscal year begins. In a larger organization, "budget preparation" time is a formalized event for the same purpose. However, there may be informal reviews by the administrator and a part of the governance board (the planning or finance committee) before a final budget is presented for approval. In a larger organization, too, the same procedures should go on among program or project directors and their staffs. The issue for large and small organizations is not the form but the regular occurrence of this particular annual planning task, with the involvement of people working in different activities and levels of responsibility. Almost everyone sees resource needs and the possibility of carrying out their work in better or new ways. That is the grist of planning and innovation. Priorities for making changes in what we do can be translated into financial priorities, and then into budget proposals which cover ongoing activities and new projects.

An annual review of activities and future plans and monthly monitoring of an approved budget are the absolute minimal tasks that a board has in carrying out the financial management requirements of its "trustee" responsibilities. The monitoring is the regular follow-up to approval of a plan of action of the organization. It is essential to the ongoing status review, a normal part of the governance activity. Since a board must approve new contracts, the consideration of a new project is a cause to review either the overall or specifically related activities of an organization. Of course, any new expenditures require prior review and approval by the board.

Quarterly or semiannual budget revisions and reviews of activities often support more effective governance and more knowledgeable backup of management and staff. They also help avoid the communication gap between staff and board that tends to grow as an organization grows. These reviews can be formal with full boards or informal among small groups of board members.

Their purpose is to be supportive and informative, and to reflect continuous review and planning.

This chapter ends with where the book began. The cycle of planning, approval, implementation, reporting, and review is complete and ready to begin again. The consciousness of this cycle and the understanding that financial management is an integral part of viewing and guiding activities will, it is hoped, make our work and organizations more productive and longer lasting.

Appendix A

Management Support Organizations

Arkansas

Independent Community Consultants, Inc.
P.O. Box 141
Hampton, AR 71744
(501) 798-4510

Primarily serves rural, southern, and minority community-based groups and community development. Special emphasis on Arkansas. Charges on sliding scale.

California

The Support Center
203 Columbus Avenue
San Francisco, CA 94133
(415) 982-4500

Provides nonprofit groups in the western part of the United States with a full range of management support services. Varying fees. (Also has office in Washington, DC.)

District of Columbia

The Community Management Center
1424 16th Street, N.W.
Suite 201
Washington, DC 20036
(202) 265-2443

Planning and Management Assistance Project
1705 DeSales Street, N.W.
Washington, DC 20036
(202) 659-1963

Provides any nonprofit organization in the Washington, DC metropolitan area. Variable fees.

The Support Center/Community Management Center
1424 16th Street, N.W.
Suite 201
Washington, DC 20036
(202) 265-2443

Provides nonprofit groups in the eastern half of the United States with a full range of management support services, paid by organization and/or resources available to organization. Variable fees. (Also has office in San Francisco.)

Illinois

W. Clement and Jessie V. Stone Foundation
111 East Wacker Drive
Suite 510
Chicago, IL 60601
(312) 564-1100

Provides free financial management services to selected nonprofit organizations throughout the United States

Michigan

Accounting Aid Society of Metropolitan Detroit
c/o New Detroit, Inc.
10 Peterboro
Detroit, MI 48201
(313) 831-0420

Accounting Aid Society of Western Michigan
8055 Lamplight Drive
Jenison, Michigan 49428
(616) 457-1076

Provides community groups in the metropolitan Detroit area and in the Grand Rapids and Kalamazoo metropolitan areas of Western Michigan, respectively, with accounting and related services. No charge.

Professional Skills Alliance
2551 John Road
Detroit, MI 48201
(313) 961-6350

Assists community organizations with accounting procedures and in applying for IRS tax-exempt status. No charge.

Minnesota

Minnesota Accounting Aid Society, Inc.
370 Hennepin Square
2021 East Hennepin Avenue
Minneapolis, MN 55413
(612) 378-1021

Provides instruction and assistance to any small nonprofit organization in the Minneapolis–St. Paul metropolitan area that cannot afford to hire professional accountant. No charge.

New York

Volunteer Urban Consulting Group, Inc.
420 Lexington Avenue
New York, NY 10017
(212) 889-4505

Works predominantly with certain designated health and social service organizations and with some groups in the arts—in the greater New York City area. No charge.

Washington

Interaction
Agency Assistance Division
1370 Stewart Street
Seattle, WA 98109
(206) 624-3272

Assists IRS, tax exempt, 501 (c) (3) organizations in Washington State referred by the Medina Foundation. No charge.

Accountants for the Public Interest

NATIONAL OFFICE

API Inc.
45 John Street
Suite 808
New-York, NY 10038
(212) 861-3836

API AFFILIATES

California
Northern California API
Fort Mason Center, Bldg. 310
San Francisco, CA 94123
(415) 771-0410

Illinois
CPAs for the Public Interest
220 South State Street, #1300
Chicago, IL 60604
(312) 786-9128

Massachusetts
Massachusetts API
44 School Street, #812
Boston, MA 02108
(617) 367-0703

New Jersey
New Jersey API
965 West Seventh Street
Plainfield, NJ 07063
(201) 755-5846

New York
New York API
36 West 44th Street, #704
New York, NY 10036
(212) 575-1828

Ohio
Toledo API
c/o Robert D. Stutz
730 Home Federal Bldg.
Toledo, OH 43606
(419) 243-3344

Oregon
Oregon API
71 S.W. Oak Street
Portland, OR 97204
(503) 225-0224

Pennsylvania
Community Accountants
1317 Filbert Street, #1008
Philadelphia, PA 19107
(215) 564-5986

Rhode Island
API of Rhode Island
Union Trust Building
170 Westminster Street, Suite 817
Providence, RI 02903
(401) 521-0710

Appendix B

Small Business Administration (SBA)
Field Offices

Aguna, GA
Albany, NY
Albuquerque, NM
Anchorage, AK
Atlanta, GA
Augusta, ME
Baltimore, MD
Birmingham, AL
Boise, ID
Boston, MA
Buffalo, NY
Casper, WY
Charleston, WV
Charlotte, NC
Chicago, IL
Cincinnati, OH
Clarksburg, WV
Cleveland, OH
Columbia, SC
Columbus, OH
Concord, NH
Corpus Christi, TX

Dallas, TX
Denver, CO
Des Moines, IA
Detroit. MI
Eau Claire, WI
Elmira, NY
El Paso, TX
Fairbanks, AK
Fargo, ND
Fresno, CA
Gulfport, MS
Harlingen, TX
Harrisburg, PA
Hartford, CT
Hato Rey, PR
Helena, MT
Holyoke, MA
Honolulu, HI
Houston, TX
Indianapolis, IN
Jackson, MS
Jacksonville, FL

Kansas City, MO
Knoxville, TN
Las Cruces, NM
Las Vegas, NV
Little Rock, AR
Los Angeles, CA
Louisville, KY
Lubbock, TX
Madison, WI
Marquette, MI
Marshall, TX
Memphis, TN
Miami, FL
Milwaukee, WI
Minneapolis, MN
Montpelier, VT
Nashville, TN
Newark, NJ
New Orleans, LA
New York, NY
Oklahoma City, OK
Omaha, NE
Philadelphia, PA

Phoenix, AZ
Pittsburgh, PA
Portland, OR
Providence, RI
Rapid City, SD
Richmond, VA
Rochester, NY
St. Louis, MO
Salt Lake City, UT
San Antonio, TX
San Diego, CA
San Francisco, CA
Seattle, WA
Sioux Falls, SD
Spokane, WA
Springfield, IL
Syracuse, NY
Tampa, FL
Washington, DC
Wichita, KS
Wilkes-Barre, PA
Wilmington, DE

For addresses and telephone numbers of the field offices listed above, consult the appropriate telephone directory.

Appendix C

SBA Publications

The free publications can be obtained from any SBA field office or from the Small Business Administration, Washington, DC 20416. The for-sale items should be ordered from the Superintendent of Documents, U.S. Government Printing Office, Washington, DC 20402. (Forms 115A and 115B list newly published releases and may be obtained without charge from SBA field or Washington, DC offices.)

Management Aids

The following are available at no charge.

85	*Analyzing Your Cost of Marketing*
169	*Designing Small Plants for Economy and Flexibility*
170	*The ABC's of Borrowing*
174	*Is Your Cash Supply Adequate?*
176	*Financial Audits: A Tool for Better Management*
178	*Effective Industrial Advertising for Small Plants*
179	*Breaking the Barriers to Small Business Planning*
181	*Numerical Control for the Smaller Manufacturer*
186	*Checklist for Developing a Training Program*
187	*Using Census Data in Small Plant Marketing*
188	*Developing a List of Prospects*
189	*Should You Make or Buy Components?*
191	*Delegating Work and Responsibility*
193	*What Is the Best Selling Price?*

Small-Business Bibliographies

The following are available at no charge.

Small-Business Management Series

The following are for sale.

Appendix D

Sources of Financial Data

In addition to information sources of the SBA, there are private sources of financial statistics. They provide data on the cost of doing business (financial ratios) in different types of enterprises and may also have information about the problems and profits of each business. Those organizations with a small-business focus are the following:

Accounting Corporation of America, an organization that provides accounting services to small business. Publishes semiannually the (Mail-Me-Monday) *Barometer of Small Business*. This ratio information is mostly about consumer businesses whose gross volume is under $500,000. For information, write: Research Department, Accounting Corporation, 1929 First Avenue, San Diego, CA 92101.

The Bank of America provides information about small businesses to students and people interested in starting them. Detailed studies and "cost of doing business" ratios are included in their *The Small Business Reporter*. Write Dept. 3120, P.O. Box 37000, San Francisco, CA.

The National Cash Register Company publishes an annual booklet entitled *Expenses in Retailing*. Other large corporations such as Eli Lilly and Eastman Kodak have information for their customers. Robert Morris Associates of Philadelphia, PA compiles much more detailed and extensive information about the costs of doing business and so does Dunn & Bradstreet, New York,

182

NY. These serve the credit evaluation needs of the banking and business communities. National trade associations also have cost information as well as industry profiles. Many publish industry magazines and newsletters in which problems and trends are discussed.

Bibliography

There are many books and professional articles on accounting and management of nonprofit organizations, but most of them apply to large structures like hospitals, universities, "welfare" organizations, cultural organizations, and foundations. Most of them are written from an accountant's point of view or in business school management language. A substantial part of such presentations is neither suitable nor meaningfully translatable to the working environment of small organizations. However, there is some published material that is useful and stimulating. It is not a substitute for accounting assistance, nor for involving people with business and managerial experience in your activities.

Accounting, Finance, and Management

BOOKS

Accounting and Financial Reporting. United Way of America, 801 North Fairfax Street, Alexandria, VA 22314, 1974.

BENNETT, PAUL. *Up Your Accountability—How to Up Your Serviceability and Funding Credibility by Upping Your Accountability.* Taft Products, Inc., 1000 Vermont Avenue, Washington, D.C. 20005.

Budgeting. United Way of America, 801 North Fairfax Street, Alexandria, VA 22314, 1975.

CONNORS, TRACY D., ed. *The Nonprofit Organization Handbook.* McGraw-Hill, Inc., 1221 Avenue of the Americas, New York, NY 10020, 1980.

GABY, PATRICIA A., and DANIEL M. GABY. *Nonprofit Organization Handbook: A Guide to Fund-Raising, Grants, Lobbying, Membership Building, Publicity, and Public Relations.* Englewood Cliffs, NJ: Prentice-Hall, Inc., 1979. Up-to-date looseleaf format.

GROSS, MALVERN J., Jr., and W. WARSHAUER, Jr. *Financial and Accounting Guide for Nonprofit Organizations.* New York: John Wiley & Sons, 1979.

HENKE, EMERSON O. *Accounting for Non-Profit Organizations.* Belmont, CA: Wadsworth Publishing Co., 1966.

National Directory of Nonprofit Management Support Organizations. The Support Center, 1709 New Hampshire Avenue, N.W., Washington, D.C. 20009.

Nonprofit Financial Management. Public Management Institute, 333 Hayes Street, San Francisco, CA 94102.

WHITAKER, FRED A. *How to Form Your Own Non-Profit Corporation in One Day: Learn How to Save Money.* Minority Management Institute, 872 69th Avenue, Oakland, CA 94621, 1979.

ARTICLES

R. MACLEOD. "Program Budgeting Works in Non-Profit Institutions." October 1971. Reprint Service, *Harvard Business Review*, Soldiers Field Road, Boston, MA 02163. Excellent for evaluating and costing activities of established organizations.

You Don't Know What You Got Until You Lose It." The Support Center/The Community Management Center, 1424 16th Street, N.W., Washington, D.C., 1976. Simple orientation material.

"Management Support Organizations." *Grantsmanship Center News*, 1031 South Grand Avenue, Los Angeles, CA 90015.

"Guide to Accounting for Nonprofit." The Grantsmanship Center, 1015 West Olympic Blvd., Los Angeles, CA 90015. Good introduction.

Index